YO-AGG-912

Teaching Tips for Religion Teachers

Teaching Tips for Religion Teachers

Grades 4-8

Richard Reichert

Our Sunday Visitor Publishing Division
Our Sunday Visitor, Inc.
Huntington, Indiana 46750

TOLL-FREE NUMBER: 1-800-348-2440

ISBN: 0-87973-365-9

PRINTED IN THE UNITED STATES OF AMERICA

Cover design by James E. McIlrath
Illustrations by Rebecca J. O'Brien

365

Contents

Introduction

Teaching Tips for Religion Teachers, Grades 4-8, is written with you, the classroom religion teacher in mind. It is based on the concept that an excellent catechist is a well-rounded catechist. A catechist needs to (1) be cognizant of the theology of the Church, (2) reflect on the meaning of that theology and apply it to his or her personal life, and (3) be able to communicate the doctrines of the Church to children in a way that is relevant to their lives.

Each chapter of *Teaching Tips for Religion Teachers* has three sections. The sections begin with CATECHETICAL REFLECTION. These brief essays encourage catechists to personalize the theme under consideration and apply it to their individual situations. The THEOLOGY UPDATE section provides a description of the Church's teachings on the topic under consideration. The final section included in each chapter is TEACHING TIPS, which offers a variety of activities that can be used with children in grades 4-8. These activities can be used equally well in parochial-school religion classes or in the once-a-week parish catechetical programs.

The activities are written with the "busy" catechist in mind. They require minimal preparation and are designed for maximum student involvement. Many of the activities have carry-over value enabling students to continue reflection at home and in the neighborhood communities.

Teaching Tips for Religion Teachers can be used effectively by individual catechists as well as parish and/or school catechists. The CATECHETICAL REFLECTION and THEOLOGY UPDATE sections provide excellent material for local in-service.

The chapter themes provide a comprehensive survey of the major themes covered in catechetical programs for grades 4-8.

Chapter 1
The Ministry of Catechesis

The ministry of catechesis is somewhat similar to the relationship of a trade master and an apprentice. In a sense, you as catechist are called upon to be a "master" Christian. Your students are apprentice Christians. Your task as master is twofold. On the one hand you seek to impart the truths, the facts, the knowledge related to our tradition. In other words, you teach doctrine. Just as important, though, you seek to develop the skills related to living out the faith in day-to-day life.

Balanced catechesis, then, not only focuses on content but also on skills development. The skills, like knowledge, develop gradually in keeping with the children's capacities and readiness. There is need for practical experiences in applying the skills. More and more personal responsibility needs to be placed on our apprentice Christians as they mature.

The actual skills related to a catechesis for Christian living have long since been identified. They were recognized by the early Church and became an integral part of the catechumenate, the official program that prepared converts for life in the Christian community. These skills include first of all a familiarity with Scripture, an ability to find one's way around Scripture, and the ability to listen to and proclaim Scripture effectively. The Bible is to the Christian what the trade manual is to an apprentice. Growing Christians must be at home with Scripture.

The second skill to be developed in our apprentice Christians is that of prayer. They not only need to know about prayer but must master the skills and arts of praying. They need opportunities to practice prayer skills with more and more regularity.

Third, our apprentices need to develop the skills related to effective participation in the liturgical life of the faith community. They must become skilled in communal worship and be able to assume a more and more active role in our liturgical celebrations.

Fourth, we need to nurture in our apprentices a highly developed moral sensitivity. That is, they must become finely attuned to the Gospel values and their implications. They must become skilled at recognizing behavior and situations that are out of harmony with Gospel values. They must also be able to apply those values to the day-to-day decisions they make.

Fifth, our apprentices must become skilled at giving witness to others of their faith in Christ. This requires practical skills in how to make Jesus and his message truly appealing to others. It also requires nurturing the courage and generosity that effective witness to others often demands.

Scripture, prayer, liturgy, morality, and witness — these are skills identified by our ancestors and considered integral to the training of converts or apprentice Christians in the catechumenate of the early Church.

Our students truly are apprentice Christians, and we as catechists are being called upon to help them develop the skills of Christian living. Knowledge alone is not enough.

Teaching Tips for Religion Teachers contains the necessary theology, reflection, child-centered activities, and resources to provide your young apprentice Christian a balanced catechesis.

THEOLOGY UPDATE

The RCIA and Catechists

The Rite of Christian Initiation of Adults (RCIA) was promulgated by the Church in 1972. Essentially this document restores and updates the process and rites of the catechumenate first developed by the Church in the fourth century. That ancient catechumenate was a kind of "apprentice" program for preparing and initiating adult converts into full membership in the Eucharistic community.

The restored catechumenate of the RCIA, like its ancient predecessor, has several central features worth noting by catechists. First, it recognizes that conversion is an ongoing process. Faith develops in stages, each involving a deepening degree of conversion. Each convert will grow at his or her own pace. So there is no rigid timeline that must be met. As in the early Church, the catechumenate experience may extend over a period of months or even years. To mark and also to promote each new stage of the catechumen's growth, the RCIA identifies an appropriate initiation rite to be celebrated. These include the Rite of Becoming a Catechumen and the Rite of Election and Enrollment, followed by the Period of

Purification and Enlightenment, which involves a series of Scrutinies and the Rite of Ephphetha (*Ephpheta* being the Greek for "Be thou opened"). The culminating celebration, of course, is the celebration of the sacraments of initiation: baptism, confirmation, and First Eucharist.

A second feature of the restored catechumenate is the vital role to be played by the catechumen's sponsor. The sponsor is asked to take an active role, representing both the convert and the faith community as a kind of bridge between the two. By word and example the sponsor is expected to encourage and to challenge the catechumen at each stage in the faith journey, up to and even beyond final initiation.

A third feature of this "apprentice" program for catechumens is the formal study of Scripture and the Creed, accompanied by training in the essential skills of Christian living: prayer and personal asceticism, liturgical participation and fellowship, Christian witness and service.

Fourth, the restored catechumenate places special emphasis on the role of the faith community itself. The local church is called upon to welcome and support the catechumens, to give them Christian example and to pray in their behalf. In other words, if the catechumens are being initiated into the Eucharistic community, that community must be visible to and concerned about them. The converts need to experience "an atmosphere of lived faith."

From that brief summary it should be evident that we catechists can learn much about our own ministry by becoming familiar with the Church's "apprentice" program for initiating converts into the faith community. In fact the four features identified above can make a quick checklist to use in evaluating our own efforts at teaching religion.

1. *Faith unfolds in stages.* Am I patient with my students and realistic in what I expect of them? Do I give sufficient recognition and seek to celebrate with them the progress they do manifest?

2. *Catechesis involves personal sponsorship.* Am I a "sponsor" in the faith development of my students? That is, do I go beyond what is required of me as a professional teacher and become personally concerned and involved in the faith development of my students?

3. *Catechesis involves both formal instruction and skills development.* Do I strive to provide balanced lessons that seek to go beyond acquiring facts about faith to develop the skills necessary for living our faith?

4. *Catechesis requires the support and witness of the entire faith community.* Do I solicit and foster that kind of support among my peers and among the parents of the children I teach?

As you can see, even as the RCIA helps us better appreciate the multiple-faceted nature of "teaching religion" it also presents us with a tremendous challenge. It challenges us to reach beyond our textbooks and into our hearts. It calls us to both practice what we teach and to teach what the children are being called to practice. It urges us to look outside the classroom to the entire faith community. But with these challenges the RCIA also gives us a consoling reminder: Growth in faith unfolds gradually and requires a series of ongoing conversions. Success doesn't require that our class be filled with saints at the end of the school year!

Chapter 2
Feasts and Seasons

Starting Off Right: Setting Realistic Goals

As we begin another school year, it might be good to bring our catechetical goals into focus once again. Stating our overall or long-range goal is easy enough. As catechists, we strive to help the children establish a personal, loving relationship with Jesus and the Father. We strive to nurture in the children the same convictions and values that animated Jesus as he proclaimed and promoted the Father's kingdom. We strive to nurture in the children an identity with and loyalty to the Church.

Being realistic, we know there are several intermediate tasks to pursue before the children can achieve that kind of faith in a mature way. We must gradually introduce the children to *facts* about Jesus and his Church. We must be careful to balance this cognitive aspect of our catechesis with concrete *experiences*. Finally, we need to provide *challenges* and *opportunities* to apply Jesus' convictions and values to everyday life. And remembering that faith is "caught" as much as it is taught, we need to continually remind ourselves of the invaluable role our own example and our tangible concern for the children play in drawing them to Jesus.

The key to translating these valid but admittedly general tasks into practical classroom goals and specific lessons is this: Know the capacities and limits of the age-group we teach. The classic principle at work here is that grace builds on nature. Even though we may translate the principle into contemporary terms, the principle remains the same. Growth in faith is related to the child's mental, psychological, and emotional growth. In the middle grades the child's faith maintains a simplicity, but it is no longer naïve. Children become interested in gathering facts about Jesus and the Church and in organizing these facts in a more systematic way. We can introduce more practical content, but we must still be careful not to demand more insight and appreciation of the truths of the Catholic faith than middle-grade children are capable of.

By junior high, these young people need and want to establish logical foundations for their faith. They feel the necessity to challenge and reject certain stories and simplistic explanations that once fully satisfied them. Nevertheless, they, too, are not ready to grasp and appreciate the mysteries of our Faith on anything near an adult level.

We must constantly adjust our goals and our catechesis to the age-group entrusted to us. The most common mistake of inexperienced catechists is to expect "too much too soon" or to "demand too little too late."

One last thought. What about you and your personal goals? What do you hope for this year? As a catechist? As a friend and disciple of Jesus? Perhaps you want to become a better storyteller or become more sensitive to each child's home situation or more comfortable in your role as prayer leader in the classroom. Why not set a goal for yourself this year, just as you refine the goals and expectations you will have for the children? If you do, though, be as realistic with yourself as you are with the children. Don't expect "too much too soon" or "too little too late."

Teaching Tips to Start the Year

Most of the activities in the TEACHING TIPS sections can be used for any of the grade levels from four through eight with minimal adaptation. Always feel free, of course, to adapt them to the needs and readiness of your students.

Introduction Trivia

Introductory games are a good way to start off a new year. They can also be a great help in getting to know your new students. Try "Introduction Trivia" for this purpose.

You'll need trivia boards (you can make your own on poster board) and dice, one set for every six students. Then make small cards cut from seven different kinds of colored paper and distribute them to the students, one set of cards to a student. Instruct the students to complete each card as follows:

Yellow Card: What is a unique or special fact about your family? (For example, Dad played college football. Grandma came from Russia.)

Green Card: What is your favorite outdoor pastime?

Blue Card: What is your birthday and birthplace?

Orange Card: What is your favorite sport?

Red Card: What is your favorite food?

Pink Card: What is your favorite TV program?
Brown Card: What is your favorite hobby?

On the back of each card, have the students print in the lower left hand corner their name or initials. Divide the class into groups and have each group sort cards according to color and shuffle them. Proceed to play according to the rules of Trivial Pursuit.

Feel free to ask different questions for each color other than the examples given. Also, this same format can be used as a drill for almost any religious education topic. With the students' help, make sets of questions on the topic you are studying at the time.

Getting Started — One

As you begin the year, this or a similar ''survey'' is a good way to get information about your students and their attitudes. Give it in one of your first classes and use the information to help your planning throughout the year:

1. What is the most important thing you learned in religion class last year?

2. What do you expect to learn in religion class this year?

3. What are some things you didn't like about religion class last year?

4. What are some things you most liked about religion class last year?

5. What would make this year's class more fun?

6. What can you do to make yourself a better student this year?

Getting Started — Two

Another approach for gathering some information about your students is the sentence-completion technique. Give the students the following list of phrases to complete:

- Kids my age are. . .
- Kids my age need. . .
- Kids my age should. . .
- For me, religion is. . .
- I believe Jesus. . .
- Going to Mass is. . .
- Religion classes are. . .
- Religion classes should be. . .
- Parents usually. . .
- The Church is. . .

Encourage the students to be honest. You can use the results in one of two ways:

1. Have the students sign the papers. Collect them and use them to give you some insights into individual students and the class as a whole.

2. Tell the students not to sign them. Collect, shuffle, and redistribute them. Begin by having each student read the first answer on the paper to the class. Then discuss together the common ideas

that emerge and summarize these on the board. Repeat the process with each question.

In this second approach, be prepared to get some facetious answers. Simply discount these without comment or go along with the humor.

Student Teacher

When you begin a new chapter, try this. Assign a group (or individual) the responsibility of giving a preview of that chapter. The group (or individual) can use this or a similar format for preparing the preview report to the class:

1. The key theme of the chapter.
2. Important new words or ideas and their definitions.
3. One way students can apply the lesson to their lives (if applicable).

To prevent or at least reduce misinformation, the students should "rehearse" their presentations ahead of time. Allow the students about five minutes to "teach" the new chapter, but you can give them more time if you feel it would be profitable.

If you prefer, you can use this approach each time you begin a new chapter, giving each student or group a chance to "teach."

The novelty of the approach heightens interest in the chapter even if the students' presentation itself isn't effective.

Variation: Assign the same chapter to several different students and allow each a few minutes to teach it. The repetition is effective. Also different students will often stress different ideas.

Profiles

At the beginning of the year, ask each student to fill out a brief personal questionnaire. It can include items like the following, but tailor it to your purposes:

- Age, height, weight.
- Names of parents.
- Address.
- Names and ages of any brothers and sisters.
- Kind and name of pet.
- Hobbies, favorite sports.
- Favorite food; least favorite food.
- Favorite singer, actor, actress.
- "Most fun-place I've visited on vacation."

Collect these, together with a snapshot of each student.

Each week, feature one student on the class bulletin board, posting the snapshot and results of the questionnaire (edited as necessary). It's a good way to make each student feel important at some point during the year. It's also a good way to help students appreciate one another. Students will look forward to seeing who will be featured each week.

Variation: For younger students, you may give the featured student certain class "privileges" that week, such as helping you pass out papers or leading the prayer service.

The Rules Are in the Bag

In the early lessons of the year, it is good to establish the rules of the classroom and reiterate the discipline policies of the program. This activity involves the students in an effort to understand the reason for the rules.

Ask each student to write one rule that every classroom should have in order for learning to take place. You may wish to assign general categories if your class is large — for example, talking, working together, assignments, the teacher, and general behavior. Collect the notes by having the students fold the notes in half and place them in a paper bag. Have the students pick one rule from the bag and try to give reasons why it is a good or bad rule for the class to follow this year. Allow others to challenge or support the individual's position. Proceed in this way until all the submitted rules are discussed.

Feel free to submit rules of your own. Then review the rules once more, choosing together those the class feels it should adopt. The final list should be printed by a volunteer on a large piece of poster board and displayed prominently in the room.

Theme for the Year

After introducing the study theme for the year and becoming somewhat acquainted with the textbook, write the theme for the year on the board. Simplify the phrase as much as possible without losing its meaning. Allow the students time to reflect on the theme, to conjure up images, phrases, symbols, songs, etc., that would make a good class motto for the year. Brainstorm and put the suggestions on the board. After some discussion, choose the theme that most students like. Examples: grade 6 — God's People in the Old Testament, Bible Buffs, Heroes — Then and Now, Bible Time Capsule.

Goal Setting: The 'Rainbow Connection'

This can be a helpful exercise for establishing some class and personal goals for the year. It's called the *Rainbow Connection* because, just as rain and sunshine interact to create a rainbow, so do dreams and realities interact to create goals.

Begin by asking the students to identify any needs they may experience this school year — for example, to be accepted, to become less shy, to get better grades. List them on the board. Then ask the students to attempt to identify some needs that you, the teacher, might have this year in the class — for example, the need for respect, the need for cooperation. You may then wish to expand to identifying needs of some other groups, such as children in lower grades, parents, the principal.

Review the list, noting overlaps where several persons or several groups of persons seem to share the same kinds of needs. Based on these kinds of needs, ask the students to help you formulate certain class goals that they all can strive to reach. For example: "We will all strive to become better listeners. We will all strive to praise one another instead of criticizing one another." Have a volunteer copy the agreed-upon goals onto a large poster board and display them prominently in the classroom.

Invitation from Jesus

The main goal of catechesis is to come to a personal relationship with Jesus, our Lord and Savior. One approach of emphasizing this aspect of our learning is to begin with an invitation exercise. Handwrite and make copies of this "letter."

> Dear _____ ,
> I'd like you to be my friend. Can you think of some time when we can get together each day? How can I tell you more about myself? Will you tell me what is important to you? Do you have any friends that we can share? I am eager to hear from you.
>
> Your friend,
> Jesus

Allow the students time to compose their letters of reply. Afterward, invite volunteers to share their letters. Help them identify common ideas all can use to respond to Jesus' invitation to friendship during the year.

A Formula for Writing Prayers

Try this formula for teaching the students to compose their own prayers — for personal and for classroom use. It's the G-R-E-A-T formula.

Greeting: Student addresses God/Jesus in a way that seems comfortable and appropriate.

Reason: Student states reason for talking to God. (I need help. I am looking for advice. I'm concerned about my dad. I'm grateful for. . . .)

Emotion or *Feeling:* Student expresses honest feelings in relation to the topic. (Fear, joy, worry, sadness, gratitude, etc.)

Action: Student expresses the action he or she would like God to take and also what he or she plans to do in relation to the topic.

Thanks: Student ends with an expression of gratitude for God's interest, past help, and anticipated help.

Have the students try out the formula by writing a prayer or two. Ask them to share these to assure that they have the right idea for each element. Encourage them to use the formula when they are praying alone. Also with practice, you can call on the students to offer spontaneous prayers for the class using the same formula. It can be used for opening or closing classes.

Get-Acquainted Acrostic

Ask each student to print the letters of his or her name vertically on a blank piece of paper. Using these letters as a starting point, ask them to express qualities about themselves. You may wish to do a sample, like the following, on the board.

en **J** oyable
g **E** ntle
N eat
frie **N** dly
sport **Y**

Challenge the students to do one with a friend's name.

S ensitive
h **U** morous
S mart
l **A** ughs
i **N** ventive

Now do a similar acrostic for Jesus your friend.

J ewish
s **E** nsitive
under **S** tands
s **U** ffered
an **S** wers prayers

Together reflect on why it seems easier to do an acrostic for ourselves or our friends than to do one for Jesus. Then ask the students to respond to these questions:

How can we get to know Jesus better as a friend?

When are some times we could spend with Jesus?

ABC's

Have the students list the letters of the alphabet down the side of a page. For each letter they must think of one word beginning with that letter related to the topic they are studying. The first student to finish wins. Or the one with the most letters completed in a set time wins.

Possible topics could include the sacraments, the Mass, the liturgical season, or the makeup of the parish. For a word to be counted the player must be able to explain what the word means, not just list it.

Variation: Using the same approach, you can open the topic to include anything related to our Catholic faith and tradition. In that case the winner is determined by who has the most words for each letter. For example, *A* — apostle, abbot, archbishop, alb. If you play in this manner it is best to form teams so that the students can help one another. Or use it as a project/homework assignment.

Spelling Bee

A good way to review and discuss words, concepts, and practices in our tradition that may not be regularly dealt with in the textbooks is this. Develop a list of words you want to teach the students — for example, rogation days, relics, thurible, scapular. Provide definitions with your list.

Have the students study the list, including the proper spelling of the words. Then hold a variation of the spelling bee. You give the definition. The student gives the word that goes with the definition and spells it. Or you give the word. The student must spell it and give the definition.

Do It Now

How often have you wished at the end of the year you had some fun snapshots of your students to use as a kind of end-of-the-year bulletin board or similar project? Start now. Make a habit of bringing your camera to class (and especially on field trips). Snap random shots both in class, before class, and between classes. Six months from now you'll be happy you did.

If you have your snaps made into slides, you can put together a fun slide show, too. You can involve students in helping with the script. But start taking those snaps now.

See What You've Learned!

At the beginning of class, present the students with a short list of questions related to what you plan to cover for that class. Go over it quickly to illustrate what the students don't yet know about the topic. Tell them to be alert for the answers to these questions as the class proceeds.

Near the end of class, go over the questions again, inviting the students to give answers. This approach does two things: (1) It heightens interest during the class. (2) It gives this age-group a much needed sense of concrete accomplishment for their efforts.

Use this approach at the beginning and ending of a new unit, too. The students can write the questions in a notebook, and as each one is answered in the following classes, they should write the answers down. They have a ready-made review to use to prepare for any test you may give at the end of the unit.

The secret, of course, is for you to prepare good questions that accurately reflect what you hope the students will learn during the class or unit.

Teaching About Advent and Christmas

Advent means arrival. In the liturgical year, Advent is a time of waiting and preparation for the arrival of the Savior. There are three kinds of "arrivals of the Savior" the Church calls to our attention during this season.

The first is the historical arrival, the birth of the Messiah two thousand years ago. We imitate the longing that the Old Testament people felt as we prepare to recall and celebrate the fact that the Messiah did indeed come. The second arrival we anticipate is the Second Coming of Jesus in glory at the end of time. This eagerly awaited arrival was probably the dominant theme of Advent in the early Church when that liturgical season first evolved. Finally, we prepare to receive Jesus into our hearts and our lives in a deeper, more intense, and renewed way today, at this moment in history.

Preparation, removing obstacles, hope, patient longing — these are attitudes the Church seeks to nurture during Advent. In the liturgical cycle, therefore, Advent is intended as a penitential time closely related to Lent.

As catechists we face a tough task as we try to nurture these attitudes in our children during the weeks preceding Christmas. To a very large degree, secular society has co-opted Christmas, promoting materialistic values instead of spiritual ones. We are all too familiar with that fact. An even greater problem is the fact that secular society, with its tendency for instant gratification, has all but destroyed Advent as a time of waiting. "Christmas" celebrating begins the day after Thanksgiving (if not sooner) when the decorations emerge and we are bombarded with Christmas music. Christmas parties often begin the first week of December in order to fit them into the busy schedule. By December 25, there is nothing left to anticipate. When the Church finally *begins* its celebration of the three arrivals of the Savior, secular society (including ourselves) is too jaded to celebrate. In such an atmosphere of premature celebrating, we clearly face an uphill struggle if we attempt to nurture the true penitential spirit of Advent in our children. Children find it hard to wait any time. Amidst the pre-Christmas hype of secular society, how do we teach Advent as a time of longing and preparing? What is there to wait for? To prepare for?

Here is one suggestion that may help us break through the effects secular society has had on the Advent season: Use Advent as a time to help the children identify and focus on all the situations that show that Jesus has not yet arrived in our midst. We have in mind those situations, locally and globally, where Jesus' absence is most clearly visible — where people do need and long for a Savior even today. In other words, use Advent as a time to focus on peace and justice issues. Where do we see strife, alienation, hatred, or loneliness locally and at large? Where are people still suffering from injustice and oppression? Where does poverty weigh people down? In short, where is salvation most needed? Who is most experiencing a deep, painful longing for a savior to free them?

We can balance this focus on Jesus' absence with the challenge to "prepare the way." That is, we can help the children identify practical things they can do during Advent to help bring Jesus' love and saving power into the lives of those most in need of it.

In this spirit, we can help children begin to understand that the "gift giving" of Christmas is actually symbolic of giving the gift of Jesus, the Savior, to others.

As catechists we are being challenged today to integrate the themes of justice and peace into our religion programs. Advent seems an ideal time to do this in a more systematic way. Peace and justice themes dominate the Scriptures for Advent, especially the Old Testament readings. The infancy narratives themselves basically proclaim a message of justice and peace.

Any practical efforts, even gestures, that we can help the children undertake to bring Christ's justice and peace to others can be most effective in catechizing them about the real meaning of both Advent and Christmas. Such efforts serve to translate the selfish and often sentimental gift-giving promoted by secular society into authentic, selfless efforts to give others Jesus' saving presence.

THEOLOGY UPDATE

The Infancy Narratives of Matthew and Luke

Probably the single most important fact to stress regarding the infancy narratives of Matthew and Luke is that they are theological in content and purpose. They are rooted in the Christology that had developed in the early Church and seek to present a particular emphasis aimed at the intended audiences of the authors. In short, they are not intended as precise eyewitness accounts, nor are they merely pious folklore intended to impress children. They are adult theology.

Matthew is writing for newly converted Jews and seeks to reinforce in them the conviction that Jesus is truly the Messiah promised and foretold in the Old Testament. His infancy narrative is consistent with this dominant apologetic that runs through his entire Gospel: Jesus fulfills all the Old Testament prophecies regarding the Messiah while the official leaders of the Jewish people remained blind to this truth through their own fault. Matthew therefore traces Jesus' genealogy back to Abraham, the Father of the Jewish people. Luke, on the other hand, is writing for newly converted Gentiles and seeks to present the Good News that Jesus is truly the Savior of all the poor and downtrodden in the world. Therefore, Luke traces Jesus' genealogy back to Adam, the father of the human race.

In Matthew the birth of Jesus is situated within the Jewish tradition and Joseph is given a central role. The comparison to Joseph of the Old Testament is obvious to Jewish converts. Joseph, husband of Mary, symbolizes all truly faithful Jews of the Old Testament, obedient to God and trustful of him. Herod and the scribes he consults, on the other hand, represent the Jewish leadership of Jesus' time: skeptical, jealous of their official position, willing to resort to deception and violence if necessary to protect their vested interests. Hence, the obstinacy that led the Jewish officials to crucify Jesus is seen to be present from the beginning. Luke, on the other hand, is careful to situate the birth of Jesus, Savior of the world, within the context of the larger world. He makes reference to Augustus Caesar and the universal power Rome then represented. The Gentiles were all too familiar with Rome and the oppressive power it utilized to achieve the Pax Romana: ". . . a decree went out from Caesar Augustus that the whole world should be enrolled" (Luke 2:1).

Matthew makes no reference to shepherds or other Jews worshiping Jesus. Rather he has the Magi visiting Jesus, representing the Gentiles who recognize and worship Jesus as Messiah even as the Jews to whom he was sent plot to kill him. The star that draws the Magi is the star of Jacob that Balaam, the famous Old Testament Magus, refers to in Numbers 24:17. Matthew also tells the story of the slaughter of the innocents and the flight into Egypt, recalling how the pharaoh, earthly ruler of another time, killed innocent children in an attempt to thwart God's saving action.

Luke does not speak of the Magi, the flight, or the massacre of the innocents, events whose Old Testament significance would have been lost on Gentiles. Instead he stresses Jesus' birth in a manger — the manger is mentioned three times — and the humble shepherds who are the first to hear the Good News and be personally invited to worship. The peace on earth that an infant in a manger is destined to bring to the poor and downtrodden is contrasted with the hollow Pax Romana that comes from opulent palaces and is enforced by brutal armies.

Foundational to both narratives is the virginal conception, which emphasizes the divine origins of Jesus. This is totally consistent with the Christology that had by then developed in the early Church and serves to reinforce that truth. It obviously has a highly apologetic purpose for both Jew and Gentile believers. Such a radical understanding was clearly an integral part of the oral tradition of the Church by that time, or it would never have been accepted by the faith community.

Even this minimal treatment of the infancy narratives should serve to demonstrate the point we seek to make. The infancy narratives are rich in Christology and need to be reflected upon in that light. We need to get beyond the sentimentality and pietisms that have come to surround the Christmas crib in popular thought. The Christmas tree is okay for little children. But the Christmas narratives of Matthew and Luke are for adults.

TEACHING TIPS

Advent Means Waiting

To help the students get into the spirit of expectation and waiting which is so central to Advent, try this.

Obtain a fairly large box. In it place either a small gift for each student or preferably some "class gift" within your power to give — for example, an envelope announcing a pizza party, a special field trip, or "three nights without homework." Whatever gift you decide upon need not be elaborate, but it should have some special meaning to your class.

Wrap the box and bring it to class the first week in Advent. Explain that it contains a gift for everyone in the class. Allow the students some time to try to guess what is in it. Comment briefly how Advent means waiting and wondering. Keep the box on display, and periodically through the season make some reference to it to sustain some sense of expectation and waiting.

Open the gift either the last class day before Christmas or the first class day after Christmas. But before opening it, relate once again the concept of waiting and hoping to the Church's own longing and waiting for Christ — two thousand years ago and also today.

Handmade Wreath

Have the students trace and cut the forms of their hands from green construction paper. On each hand, print one way that they will help their family prepare for Christmas. Assemble the green hands in the shape of a wreath. (Hands can be glued to a round pizza cardboard.) Add real or paper-tube candles. Tape to the candle the prayer that the class will say that week as their special Advent prayer. (For example: Week 1 — meal prayer; Week 2 — Hail Mary; Week 3 — Our Father; Week 4 — Creed.)

Let Your Light Shine

Advent wreaths need four candles. Make class (community) Advent candles. Ask each student to bring candle stubs or canning wax from home. Wicks and molds can be purchased from craft stores. Place the stubs into an old pan on a hot plate. Melt the wax and add bits of purple crayons for color. Pour the mixture into small milk cartons or containers from a craft store.

For the more ambitious, a good experience in practicing patience would be to dip the Advent candles for your wreath. The same wax-collecting process could be followed. Pour the wax into a tall, slender container. A coffee can will work nicely. Attach the wicks to a ruler. Allow each student a turn at dipping and holding the candles. To save time, you may wish to start with tapers and add new layers of wax.

Jesse Tree: Past and Present

Assign each student a traditional biblical member of God's family. Pass out paper circles and markers. Instruct the class to draw a symbol for that person or describe, in a word or phrase, that person's contribution to preparing for Jesus' coming. Glue the circles to felt or construction-paper backing. Pass out a second circle to each student. Have the students draw a symbol or print a word describing their *own* Advent contribution. Attach all symbols to the class Jesse Tree — usually a bare twig.

Cookies for the Hungry

With the assistance of room aides (mothers), prepare several batches of a basic sugar-cookie recipe. Ask each student to bring his or her favorite Christmas cookie cutter from home. Get several volunteers to bring frosting and sprinkles. Begin the class with cutting and baking the cookies. Frost and decorate the cookies, then sell them to the other classes. Be sure to announce the sale the week before so that the students will remember to bring money. Explain that the money will go to a needy family in the parish for Christmas food and gifts. The money could also be sent to a relief organization for the starving peoples of the world.

Learning to Wait

Discuss situations in which students are made to wait — cafeteria lines, shopping lines, lines for buses, etc. What often happens when we wait? How could waiting become a positive experience? Ask each student to suggest something positive to do when waiting. Write this suggestion on a slip of paper. Collect all slips in a container marked CAN OF PATIENCE. Ask each student to choose one slip from the can and try to practice patience that week. The next week, collect the slips from those who successfully achieved patience. Allow them to choose another *patient practice* for the following week. At the end of Advent, tie a bow on the CAN OF PATIENCE and offer it to the Lord in a class prayer service.

Remember to Be Bearers of Good News (Isaiah 52:7)

Many people send Christmas cards with personal messages before Christmas. They are usually full of good news and sent to friends and relatives. Discuss with the class the effect of such warm messages at Christmastime. Who are the people who seldom receive messages of cheer, whose services are often overlooked or taken for granted? (Postman, parish janitor, cafeteria cooks in school, etc.) Have each student think of someone who could use some good news. Use old Christmas cards and construction paper to fashion personalized Christmas greetings for these people who are often forgotten. Provide envelopes for the students and encourage them to hand deliver these messages.

An Italian Christmas Custom

One of the traditions among Italian families is that of the children writing a letter to their parents thanking them for all that they have done for them. The letter is placed under the plate of the father or mother to be opened on Christmas Day. Assist the class in writing Christmas letters of thanks to their parents, adding designs from old Christmas cards. Sincere thanks is a gift well appreciated.

Variation on Advent Calendar

December is a hectic month, and tensions rise with the coming holidays. Pass out blank December calendars. Ask the class to fill in the tasks and events that will take place in their family before Christmas (Christmas shopping, concerts, parties, and visiting). Challenge the students to leave these calendars in their bedrooms and keep them up-to-date by doing the following: (1) Place a large "X" on the dates when they contributed to the tension of the day. (2) Cover the days in yellow or with a Christmas sticker if they helped the family maintain a positive spirit.

Variation of the Kris Kringle Custom

Have each student pick a name from a box containing the names of all the students in the class. Be sure no one gets his or her own name. Keeping the name confidential, ask the students to make an effort to get to know the person whose name they chose during the Advent season. At the last class before Christmas, ask the class to write a letter to the student that they got to know better, describing the good qualities they discovered and wishing that individual a Merry Christmas. Positive reinforcement is sometimes the best gift we can give one another.

Collect Good Deeds

Decorate a shoebox like a Christmas gift. Challenge the class members to come in with a written paragraph of a good deed or helpful event they initiated during the week. Seal these paragraphs with a Christmas sticker of the student's choice. During the final class before Christmas, have each student choose a good-deed slip from the box and read it to the class. This can be part of a prayer service focusing on the praise and glory we give to God with our lives. Close by singing together "Angels We Have Heard on High."

Peace on Earth

Pass out patterns of a dove on white paper. Have the students print their names on the front. On the back of the dove, print a way in which each feels that he or she can be a peacemaker among his or her friends or in the family. Hang the doves on a small (real or artificial)

Christmas tree. Read the passages from Isaiah announcing the coming of the Prince of Peace. The song "Let There Be Peace on Earth" is also appropriate.

It Is in Giving That We Receive

Christmas gifts for needy children are often used toys and unwanted games. Ask the class to pick a slip for a Christmas exchange. The slip should give the first name and age of a needy child of the parish or the gender and age of the child. Instruct the students to buy a gift costing in the neighborhood of three to five dollars, wrap it, and label it. The day usually scheduled for the class gift exchange could be a presentation of the gifts to a representative of the St. Vincent de Paul Society or the Salvation Army.

A New Kind of Advent Wreath

Advent is more than a time to prepare for the celebration of the birth of Jesus in history. It is also a time of longing for the kingdom of God in its fullness at the Second Coming of Jesus. To teach this vital dimension and give Advent a practical focus, try this as a change from the traditional Advent wreath.

Prepare a wreath but instead of the traditional candle get these four "kingdom" symbols ready to put on it:

First Week: Dove or other *Peace* Symbol.

Second Week: Scale or other *Justice* Symbol (for example, bread).

Third Week: A Ring or other *Unity* Symbol.

Fourth Week: Gospels or other Symbol announcing the *Good News*.

Develop a short prayer around each week's "kingdom" theme, together with a Scripture passage suitable to that theme. Begin each week with your prayer service and place the symbol for that week on the wreath. Challenge the students during the week to do specific works intended to bring about that aspect of the kingdom for which we long. You may wish to have them help you compile a list of possible good works related to each theme. Make the lists as practical as possible.

Mary Candle

Advent is the Church's time to recognize Mary and her "yes" in our salvation. Apart from the sentimental role often assigned to Mary, her strong "yes" allowed all of us to be redeemed. Use the Sunday Scripture readings for the four Sundays and discuss how Mary exemplified the whole period of expectation, and the virtues and values necessary to be ready for the Savior. A concrete symbol of this period is the Mary candle. Use a tall candle holder and drape over it a white cloth symbolizing Mary as the tabernacle of the Most High. The candle can be lit at prayer times or during the evening meals.

A Holy Babe

Christmas is the season that fills our thoughts with scenes of the Holy Baby, Jesus. Intermediate and junior-high students often baby-sit for many not-so-blessed tykes. In the true spirit of Christmas, challenge the older students to accept a regular baby-sitting appointment and then to do it for free in honor of the Father who sent his only Son as a babe for the salvation of the world.

Liturgical Cycle Game

Make a simple game board by drawing a large circle on a piece of poster board. In pie fashion divide the circle into the liturgical seasons: Advent, Christmas/Epiphany, Lent, Easter, and Pentecost. Remember to interspace the periods of Ordinary Time after Christmas/Epiphany and after Pentecost. Use a soda straw and pin to make a spinner for the board. As an added feature you may want to color each section with the appropriate liturgical color.

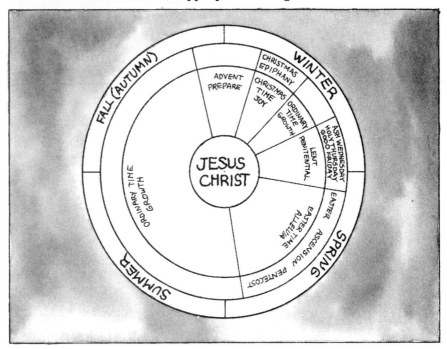

After you have studied the seasons, have the students make up a number of questions related to each season and write these on 3'' x 5'' cards; for example, for Advent: How many weeks does Advent contain? Name a famous prophet of the Old Testament whose message we read during Advent. What is Gaudete Sunday?

Form teams. Have the teams spin the pointer and then answer a question related to the season pointed to. Keep score. The teams with the most correct answers win.

Variation: You can use this same approach to review the parts of the Mass. Design the board accordingly and develop the questions related to the parts of the Mass.

Teaching About Lent

Today's children — and most catechists under thirty — have no personal experience or memory of what Lent was like in the days before Vatican II.

Those of us whose adult life bridges the pre- and post-Vatican II era can remember things like a stash of stale candy, much of it stuck together and covered with lint, that was stored in some drawer to be reclaimed at 12:01 on Holy Saturday afternoon. The haunting melody of the "Stabat Mater" is embedded.in our memories and its refrain can still conjure up feelings associated with the Lents of our childhood and youth. Even putting nostalgia aside, we "old-timers" can say with certitude that people took Lent more seriously in the past. It seemed to have a significance in the life of the Church that has been lost in the aftermath of the Second Vatican Council renewal.

In helping our children — and ourselves — rediscover this most solemn season of the Church's year we need to be careful to keep our catechetical goals clear. Lent has its origins and derives its meaning as a preparation time for the celebration of the New Passover, the triduum feast of Jesus' passion, death, and resurrection and the mystery of our redemption in him. That is the first thing we should strive to impress upon our children. The ancient triduum is the high point of the Church's year, just as it is the high point of salvation history. The liturgical cycle revolves around these mysteries of our redemption and derives its meaning from them. Appreciating the triduum, and by extension all of Holy Week, as the focal point of the Church's life and its liturgical year, is the foundation our children will need before they can enter into the authentic spirit of Lent and its traditional practices: fasting, almsgiving, and prayer. This is a bit more difficult than it may at first appear. Secular society has made Christmas the focal point of its year (and proceeded to bury it in crass materialism and commercialism). Children can sing ten Christmas carols from memory for every Easter hymn. "Jingle Bells" is learned before the "Alleluia."

Theologically we have no difficulty demonstrating that the triduum is *the* feast of the Church year. Psychologically and emotionally, however, it will be an uphill climb to impress this fact on children today.

To the degree that we succeed, we can then present the forty-day period of preparation for this feast in its proper perspective, the second goal of our catechesis. The traditional way to prepare for Easter is by a program of fasting, almsgiving, and prayer. All three are integrally related and support one another. Before we challenge our children to undertake specific practices, however, we must first help them grasp the purpose behind these traditional disciplines.

These practices are not intended as a means of paying back to God some debt we have incurred by our sinfulness. That concept focuses on our sins rather than Jesus' redemption. This misunderstanding immediately connotes a quantitative approach. It focuses on the practices instead of their end. We must help the children see almsgiving as a means of overcoming our selfishness so we can be attentive to and reconciled to the needs of our brothers and sisters. Our prayer is aimed at restoring and deepening our communion with God. Asking for forgiveness is but one aspect of this attempt to relate more intimately with God. Fasting frees us from our preoccupation with and potential enslavement by the needs and pleasures of our flesh. Thus freed we are able to be more attentive to our neighbor and our God.

Now we are ready for the third goal of a catechesis for Lent: helping children identify and develop a functional program of Lenten practices. For the early Church, Lenten fasting meant first of all "fasting from sin." It is a time to turn from selfish habits that alienate us from our neighbor and God. Then and only then will specific disciplines like "giving up something" take on meaning. What we choose to "give up" should be as much as possible associated with selfish practices and excesses. "Giving up" TV, for example, would probably be a more wholesome form of fasting for today's children than "giving up" candy. For children, almsgiving should probably take the form of giving additional service and time to their neighbor, rather than money or other goods. If the purpose of almsgiving is reconciliation and care for our neighbor, physically reaching out to the one next to us can have more value than putting twenty-five cents in the mission box. That form of literal almsgiving should still be encouraged, of course, but only in the context of a broader understanding of the purpose of all almsgiving.

Lent as a special time of prayer can best be approached by reestablishing some of the traditional Lenten devotions like the Stations of the Cross. Children will need the help of such structured prayer experiences, but we should encourage them to go beyond formal prayers to personal prayer time. Lent, therefore, is the ideal time for a more intense and systematic catechesis on prayer.

We can never recapture the "old-fashioned Lent" of the past. We should not strive to. We can hand on to our children, however, that appreciation for Jesus' passion, death, and resurrection that is the source for understanding Lent. We can nurture an authentic tradition of fasting, prayer, and almsgiving and help the children give expression to that tradition in new ways.

███████████████████████████████

Lent

If you were to unroll a huge snowball lying at the base of a mountain you would have a fairly accurate record of what lies on the side of the mountain, from bottom to top. And at its core you would find the small, unchanged stone around which that record formed. It is much the same if we attempt to study the development of Lent through the ages to the present day. It contains a record of the Church's developing theology through the ages, including some of its meanderings. At its core is the unchanged mystery that started it all: the Paschal event of Jesus' passion, death, and resurrection. What follows is just a sample of what that record would reveal.

Lent started as a triduum feast: Good Friday, Holy Saturday, and Easter Sunday. This celebration recalled and re-presented for the early Christians the core event of the Good News, our redemption achieved by Jesus' passion, death, and resurrection. Very early this central feast of the Church began to include the commemoration of the Last Supper, or Holy Thursday. Then it became the week of the Lord's passion, death, and resurrection.

Appropriately, this week commemorating our redemption soon became the time for two major events in the life of the Church. On Holy Thursday public sinners were reconciled to the community. Also, converts were baptized, confirmed, and brought to the Eucharistic table during the Easter Vigil.

Next the Church began to prepare for this holiest of weeks by three weeks of fasting. By the fourth century the period of preparation was extended to forty days. Ash Wednesday became the day public sinners enrolled in a formal period of fasting and penance in preparation for their reconciliation on Holy Thursday. Catechumens, after a training period of up to three years, began the final days of preparation for initiation into the community.

The readings at the liturgy began to reflect the major themes of salvation history, from the creation and fall through the Exodus and covenant experience to the final days of Jesus' life and the New Passover. The dominant themes became the call to conversion and repentance in response to God's invitation to new life in Jesus. Baptism imagery abounded.

By the Middle Ages the practice of public penance had fallen into disuse. Infant baptism had replaced the practice of adult preparation through a catechumenate. Lent was no longer viewed as a special period of preparing individuals for joining the faith community. Rather Lent had become a time of personal penance for the universal Church. Everyone, not just public sinners, submitted to the Ash Wednesday ritual of enrollment into a program of penance, publicly acknowledging his or her sinfulness and need for reconciliation. Gradually the readings for the liturgical services began to reflect this new emphasis, de-emphasizing the theme of baptism and salvation history. This continued into the twentieth century.

As a result of the work of Vatican II and the restoration of the adult catechumenate, Lent is once more viewed as the final stage in the preparation of catechumens for the sacraments of initiation. The "A Cycle" readings reflect the more ancient selection of readings used during Lent to prepare catechumens. The "B" and "C Cycles" reflect the expansion of the Church's concept of Lent as a time of penance for the universal Church.

If Jesus' passion, death, and resurrection constitute the unchanging theological core around which Lent developed, then prayer, fasting, and almsgiving are the unchanging ascetical practices of preparation for the triduum feast.

These practices were seen as correlative by the early Church. St. Augustine says in one of his Lenten sermons, "By almsgiving and fasting we add wings of fervor to our prayers so they more easily fly and reach God." St. Leo says, "Let fasting Christians grow fast through the distribution of alms and care to the poor." Another time Augustine says, "When the soul is freed from the burden of excessive food and drink, it comes to know itself better . . . and realizes how devotedly it should follow the Redeemer."

For the Fathers of the Church the three practices represented a balanced asceticism aimed at restoring and deepening our union with God and one another: prayer aimed at union with God. Fasting freed us from selfish preoccupations and overconcern for the flesh so that we might better attend to the needs of our brothers and sisters by almsgiving and so that we could turn to God in prayer.

The goal was to reclaim the peace and reconciliation with God and our neighbor that Jesus had already won for us. The idea of "winning forgiveness" was foreign to the early Christian community and to the Church Fathers. Conversion from sin rather than "paying for sins" was central.

Gradually, however, the ascetical practices became ends themselves. They became canonical duties rather than freely willed responses to God's invitation to return and to enter more deeply into the mystery of our redemption.

Prayer, fasting, and almsgiving became separated and isolated acts rather than organically related facets of the same response to God's invitation. They became unintelligible burdens to some. They became self-inflating exercises to others.

These misunderstandings accumulated around the core of Lent through the centuries, but the true meaning of Lent and Lenten practices endured along with these.

Today we are in the process of stripping away the misunderstandings and uncovering the core meaning of Lent. Lent once more is seen as a time of preparation for the celebration of our redemption. We prepare as did the early Church by turning from selfishness and discord through the practices of almsgiving, fasting, and prayer.

Preparing for Lent

Explain that the spirit of Lent is traditionally a time to repair and to renew our relationships — with God, with our neighbor, with ourselves. It involves these three kinds of practices:

Prayer — attending to and deepening one's relationship with God by spending more time being with him, listening to his word, talking to him.

Almsgiving — includes any works of charity we do for others that seek to repair the relationship with our neighbor that sin has wounded.

Fasting — involves any acts of self-denial that can be used to root out the selfishness that causes us to ignore God and treat our neighbor badly.

1. Now invite the students to develop their own Lenten-Practice Card. Supply each student with a 5'' x 7'' index card. It should be divided into three headings as follows:

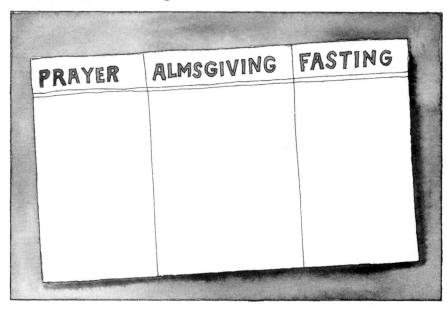

2. Help them think through and identify one or more *realistic* things they do in each column.

3. They should translate these into their own kind of code or shorthand and copy them onto their card.

4. Encourage them to put this card on their mirror at home, in a book they use every day or in some other place where it will serve as a daily reminder.

5. Part way through Lent, ask them to bring in their cards. Invite them to share how they are doing and allow time for them to come up with alternative ideas if the present ones don't seem to be working.

6. Collect the cards the week before Easter and develop a little

prayer service during which these are offered to God by the students as their Lenten gift.

Variation: You can do this activity as a class. Have the entire class identify a class project of prayer, almsgiving, and fasting. Then have the students construct a poster and display it as a class reminder of what they have committed themselves to do during Lent.

A Lesson Plan for Lent

The following can help your students form an understanding of Lent and its traditional components:

1. Have the students draw this diagram on a sheet of paper or poster board:

2. Make a large poster like the above for the entire class. (Better yet, ask for volunteers to make the poster.)

3. Explain as follows:

√ The forty days of Lent are a time to prepare for the celebration of Easter.

√ At Easter we celebrate Jesus' victory over sin and death. We celebrate our redemption from the hatred and alienation our selfishness causes. We are restored to friendship with God and our neighbor. *We are born!*

√ The basic practice of Lent is fasting. We fast or turn away from any sinful or selfish habits and attitudes we may have. We fast from unnecessary things and practices that focus only on ourselves and our own pleasure (self-indulgence).

√ Fasting *frees* us to have extra time for God. We are free to spend more time in praying and talking to God, getting to know him better. We are free to restore and develop our friendship with God.

√ Fasting also frees us to spend more time being aware of our neighbors and their needs. We are free to help them. We can heal friendships that our selfishness has wounded.

4. Have the students share their ideas on the following (list on the board):

   √ The kinds of "sin" and selfishness that are common for their age-group that cause them to become alienated from God and one another.

   √ "Fasting" appropriate for the age-group. This should be in relation to the kinds of selfishness they identified — for example, gossiping, fighting with brothers and sisters, teasing, littering, and not doing chores well. Ideas for "fasting" should also be directed toward "overindulgence" in good things, including watching TV and spending money on video games, junk food, etc.

   √ Spending more time at prayer: When and where, kinds of prayer that would be good, devotions that could be developed. Encourage them first of all to work at improving existing practices such as being more attentive at Mass, morning and evening prayers, meal prayers, class prayers.

   √ "Almsgiving." These should take the form of service and help, but can include some specific monetary donations. For instance, money saved from cutting down on video games can be given to some specific charity.

5. Direct the students to choose one or more practices from each of the lists and write them on their personal Lent diagrams on the lines provided. Encourage them to keep these in some private place but where it will also serve as a personal reminder to them: on the inside of the closet door in their room, pasted on the inside cover of their notebook, etc.

6. Now have the class, using the large class poster, identify some class practice for each of the three Lenten Practice categories. For example — (a) "fast" from cruel forms of teasing one another; (b) pray a decade of the rosary together each day for world peace; (c) collect money for a certain number of weeks to be given to some charity at the end of Lent.

Thirty-Second Theology

The Collect for the daily Mass each day during Lent continually reflects the spirit of Lent and maintains a proper focus on the purpose of our Lenten practices. It would be a good prayer to start class each day during Lent. Occasionally you can take time to discuss and reflect on the theology a particular Collect contains and incorporate it into a lesson plan.

The Cross in Tradition

The Cross, being the special symbol of Christianity, has been expressed in various shapes through the ages. Each shape has its own significance and history. Have your students research and prepare reports on each of the following:

- Latin Cross.
- Jerusalem (Crusader's) Cross.
- St. Andrew's Cross.

- Maltese Cross.
- Greek Cross.
- Papal Cross.
- Anchor Cross.

As an art or craft project the students can make posters of each of the crosses. Or they can fashion the various crosses out of putty, heavy cardboard, styrofoam, etc.

Dying and Rising

Fashion a miniature casket out of a shoebox. On slips of paper have the students write one bad habit they will seek to "bury" during Lent. Make sure they do not sign the slips. On the first day of Lent hold a mock funeral. Have the students file past the casket and place their slip in it. Put the lid on the casket and "bury" it inside a larger box designed to look like a tomb. (You can involve the students in making the casket and the tomb.)

Sometime during Lent remove the slips and read them without the students' knowledge.

Make "resurrection" slips, with the reverse of the bad habit on them. "Fighting with older sister," for example, is transformed into "Being kind to older sister." These "resurrection" slips should be written on some appropriately decorated note paper or cards reflecting the Easter theme. Among possibilities are a lily, the word Alleluia, and cardboard pieces in the shape of butterflies.

On the first class after Easter have the opened tomb prominently displayed. Have the lid off the casket inside. Pin on the bulletin board or in various places around the room the "resurrection" slips. Allow the students to try to find their own, but they should not remove them. Keep them on display for a suitable time after Easter.

Words of Encouragement

Find out from the pastor the names and addresses of any catechumens who are preparing to be baptized at the Easter Vigil. Have the students write short notes to them explaining that they are praying for them during Lent and the time of their preparation.

Words of Thanks

Have the students make Easter cards for their godparents. They should include in them a note thanking them at this time of the year when we all recall and thank God for our baptism.

In Absentia

Many children never attend the Easter Vigil for various reasons. To ensure that they begin to become familiar with this most solemn and beautiful of our liturgies, use several sessions prior to Easter to walk them through the prayers and readings. Given the length of these it is best to take them in smaller sections. Devote, for instance, one session to the Light Ceremony and the blessing of the Paschal Candle and the Font. The "Exultet" can be studied in one session. Devote one session to the Salvation History readings. Another session can be devoted to the petitions and their significance. The Baptism Ceremony and the renewal of Baptismal Vows can be reviewed.

Variation 1: Assign various portions of the ceremony to different groups. Have each group prepare a report and/or demonstration of their portion of the liturgy.

Variation 2: Using Holy Week missalettes, have the students develop posters outlining the ceremonies for Holy Thursday, Good Friday, and the Easter Vigil.

Another Approach to the Stations

Write on the board and discuss each Station of the Cross in turn, in two parts:

1. Using the Gospel accounts, discuss what actually happened and what Jesus and the other people involved might have been thinking and feeling. Discuss motives where appropriate.

2. Then attempt to identify *generic* sins related to that station and acts of virtue or concern that counteract those kinds of sins. For example, at the first station, Jesus is condemned to death. Sins might include rash judgment and prejudice. Virtues might include tolerance, patience, and compassion for the imprisoned.

You may wish to take several sessions to do this to ensure enough time for the students to discuss and really enter into the drama, tragedy, and meaning involved in each of the stations.

As you complete your discussion of each station, come to an agreement on key ideas, and record these.

When you have completed all fourteen stations, divide the class into groups and assign each group one or more of the stations. Provide them with the summaries of discussion for the stations assigned to them. Each group then prepares a short reflection or prayer for that station. You may want to provide the groups with copies of a traditional Stations of the Cross booklet to use as a guide for the format of the reflection or prayer they compose.

On a suitable day during Lent go to the church and pray the stations. Have each group lead the prayer for the station (or stations) assigned to it.

Variation: You might want to invite parents or another class to join you in the prayer service.

Finally, as Easter nears, discuss the resurrection account as the "fifteenth station."

Each of the original groups is then asked to develop its own reflection or prayer for this fifteenth station.

After Easter, each group in turn leads the class in its reflection or prayer on a different day until all have had their chance. This is a good way to give special focus to the "Easter event" and to prolong its celebration through the Easter season.

Lenten Lesson

A simple way to explain the central purpose of Lent is through the image of the Cross. Start by stating that the overall theme and goal of Lent is to heal relationships or to restore unity and peace with God, with our neighbor, and with ourselves. Then present a diagram of the Cross (see illustration below):

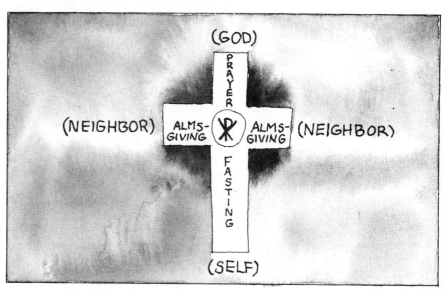

Explain that the three main practices of a Christian during Lent are prayer, almsgiving, and fasting. By fasting, we seek to root out whatever selfishness we have that keeps us trapped within ourselves. By almsgiving, we seek to reach out to our neighbor and heal broken relationships our selfishness may have caused. And through prayer, we seek to reach toward God and deepen our relationship with him. Jesus is represented by the circle at the center of the Cross. All our Lenten activities are done in his name. It is in and through Jesus that relationships are ultimately healed and that peace and unity are restored.

Adapt this explanation to the age-group you are teaching. Then help them translate the notion of prayer, almsgiving, and fasting into specific kinds of practices suitable for their age.

For example, almsgiving is sharing our time, our talents, our concern, our interest, (and our treasure) with our neighbor. Using the students' suggestions, list a number of possible ways they could "give alms" this Lent.

As another example, fasting means doing things that will help us be more attentive to God and our neighbor. Some suggestions could include watching less TV; taking money that might be wasted on junk food or video games and donating it to the missions or other charity; using some time that is normally spent listening to records and using it for prayer or for helping someone else.

Encourage the students' creativity — and practicality — in developing such a list of possible practices. Then have each student draw a cross on an 8½" x 11" sheet of paper. They should write in the words PRAYER, ALMSGIVING, and FASTING, as shown in the diagram above. Then next to each arm of the cross they should list one or two practices in each category that they plan to carry out this Lent. Hold a short "commitment service" during which the students sign their names to their sheets as a pledge that they will seek to carry out these practices. Suggest that they hang these commitment sheets in their rooms at home as a daily reminder.

Remind them periodically during Lent about their commitment sheet and invite the students to share any successes or failures they may be experiencing. Remind them also that the test of the effectiveness of their practices is better relationships with their parents, with their brothers and sisters, with their classmates, with themselves, and ultimately with God.

Relating the Stations of the Cross to Life

Try this. With student help, make fourteen plain posters, each with the title of one of the Stations of the Cross on it, and a simple cross at the top.

Hang these simple posters around the room in order. Take a class or a portion of a class to review the events surrounding each station. In the process, carefully explain how the effects of sin and the suffering of Jesus continue today in the lives of the people around us. Cite some concrete examples — for instance, innocent men, women, and children who have contracted AIDS and are "condemned" to death as a result (First Station); people like Mother Teresa of Calcutta who care for the dying (Sixth Station); persons addicted to drugs or alcohol who are struggling to rise from their addiction (Third, Seventh, or Ninth Station).

Invite the students to try to relate the events of each station to real-life suffering in today's society.

Ask the students to keep an eye out for newspaper or magazine articles and pictures that somehow relate to one or another of the Stations of the Cross. When they find one, they are to bring it in and tape it to the appropriate station. You may wish to "prime the pump" by bringing in several yourself to give them a feel for what they are looking for.

Encourage them to continue this throughout Lent, so that by the end of the season each station is well-represented with contemporary examples of the suffering of Jesus and the effects of sin. This exercise can greatly heighten student sensitivity.

Periodically during Lent, pray the stations in class (or pray one station each day). Help the students reflect not only on the love and courage of Jesus but also invite them to pray for the victims whom they have identified in relation to a particular station.

CATECHETICAL REFLECTION

Teaching About Easter

If we were asked to boil all catechesis down to one word, that word would have to be *Easter*. All other events of Jesus' life and all other truths revealed by God and expressed in our creed derive their meaning from our belief in Jesus' resurrection.

Jesus' resurrection was the core of the Good News the Apostles so enthusiastically proclaimed. Acceptance of the faith the Apostles taught depended directly upon belief in Jesus' resurrection. As Paul said, ". . . if Christ has not been raised, your faith is vain; you are still in your sins. Then those who have fallen asleep in Christ have perished. If for this life only we have hoped in Christ, we are the most pitiable of men" (1 Corinthians 15:17-19).

Ironically, for us twentieth-century catechists, too much faith in the resurrection rather than too little faith may be our problem. If we were raised from infancy in the Christian tradition, the truth of Jesus' resurrection and our personal immortality were probably always an integral part of our approach to life — and death. In short, we probably take resurrection and immortality for granted.

For that reason, it can be hard for us to experience and enter into the spirit of total astonishment and overwhelming joy that were contained in the Apostles' preaching and expressed so beautifully in the liturgies of the Easter season. An analogy might help. If you have always been able to see, it is very difficult to appreciate the joy and astonishment of a person born blind who later gains sight. It is hard to imagine what it must be like to see a sunrise, a rose, a kitten, or a strawberry for the first time at age eighteen or thirty-eight. Blessed with sight and gifted with such images since infancy, we take these wonders (that's what they are) for granted.

In much the same way, try to imagine what it would be like to have lived all one's life in a world that is fatalistic. No hope for personal immortality. No hope for ultimate delivery from evil, injustice, suffering, and oppression. No real sense that one's personal existence has any meaning beyond the immediate pleasure or pain one is experiencing. Then along comes a group who tells you the Good News that all evil, that death itself, has been conquered. The group tells you that through Jesus your wildest dreams and most far-fetched fantasies about everlasting life and eternal happiness are no longer fantasies but realities within reach. You are a unique, special person with a personal everlasting destiny! Astonishment, joy, and hopeful enthusiasm seem to be the most common characteristics of the first proclaimers and the first believers in this Good News.

As catechists, we are proclaimers and explainers of the same Good News. Imagine how effective we can become in our ministry if we can reclaim and sustain that same kind of personal astonishment and joy in the wonder and significance of Jesus' resurrection. Imagine the effect on the children if we can proclaim and explain the Good News with the same kind of personal, heartfelt enthusiasm that literally drove the Apostles to share the Good News with all who would listen.

Easter season is a special time for entering once again into the mystery of Jesus' resurrection. It is the ideal time to seek to experience something of the astonishment and overwhelming joy that the meaning of Jesus' resurrection contains.

In the same way, it is no accident that the Church regards each Sunday's liturgy as a commemoration and re-celebration of Easter. In a real sense, the Church celebrates Easter every week of the year. The Church itself is most aptly described as an Easter people. The event of Easter is the very source of our identity.

It is not an exaggeration to suggest that the overall effectiveness of our teaching will be in more or less direct proportion to the Easter-motivated enthusiasm we bring to our daily task of sharing this Good News with the children. You can't fake enthusiasm, least of all with children. On the other hand, nothing is more readily caught by children than one's honest enthusiasm.

So if Easter is what we ultimately teach, Easter enthusiasm is our most effective method. May you reclaim it this Easter season, and sustain it throughout the year.

THEOLOGY UPDATE

Alleluia! Jesus Is Risen

Believing *that* Jesus was raised from the dead is one thing. Understanding *what* this resurrection was like is quite another. We can be sure of this much: Jesus' return from death was radically different from the experiences of those revived from "death" or who had an "out of body" experience and were then revived by techniques like CPR (cardiopulmonary resuscitation).

As dramatic and profound as these experiences are, such people undergo no real change in their bodies. There is no physical transformation. After revival, they continue to be subject to all the limits we associate with physical bodies, including vulnerability to future sickness, pain, and ultimately death.

Jesus' own resurrection is obviously different. The Gospels make that clear — in the very picture of confusion they present. The authors could draw on no human words or past human experience to accurately express the Apostles' encounters with Jesus in his resurrected state. Simply put, he was different, yet the same Jesus who was crucified, died, and had been buried a few days before. They experienced a *transformed* Jesus, not simply a Jesus who was *revived* from death. This transformation was so complete that the

Apostles had trouble recognizing him at first. They were startled not merely *because* he appeared to them after death, but *how* he appeared to them after death.

Perhaps the best way to attempt to describe this transformation is to say that Jesus' body had become *enspirited*. That is, the corporeal dimension of Jesus' humanity had taken on all the qualities we tend to use to describe spiritual reality. His body was no longer subject to the limits of matter, such as time, space, weight, and solidity. Jesus' sudden appearances and disappearances testify to this. His body had taken on the qualities of spirit. Time, space, pain, and death itself no longer had *power* over his body.

Yet, Jesus' body paradoxically continued to be *flesh*. He was no mere disembodied specter or ghost. His Apostles could see him, touch him, hear him in all the tangible ways we associate with embodied persons. They could walk with him, talk with him, embrace him, eat with him. He could continue to identify with all our earthly needs, even to the extent of building a fire and cooking breakfast for his disciples.

Of all the things to ponder in confronting this mystery, we'd like to focus on two. First, it seems important for us to realize that Jesus continues to exist in his enspirited flesh in the same way he appeared to his Apostles after his resurrection. Jesus' incarnation is forever! This Eternal Word has chosen to continue his eternal existence *incarnated* in our human nature. What dignity this bestows on us enfleshed beings!

Second, our own bodies have that same capacity to be transformed, to become fully enspirited like Jesus. Contrary to certain popular piety in the past, our body is not something we are entrapped in, a burden we seek to shed in order to enjoy a more spiritual existence. Our bodies participate in our journey toward fullness and perfection. Like Jesus, we are destined to spend eternity as incarnate beings, embodied persons.

On a very practical level, meditation on the nature of Jesus' resurrection should lead us to an ever more profound reverence for our bodies and for the entire material universe, which in a real sense is an extension of our bodies.

Matter in general (and particularly the human body) is not an afterthought on God's part. Our body should not be viewed as some burden or as an obstacle to growth intended only to test us on our spiritual journey. Our body is integral to our being. It defines who we are and what we are intended to be through all eternity.

Of course, as we journey to perfection, our bodies can seem to be a burden, and we tend to experience ourselves as entrapped spirits. At our own resurrection, however, we will experience our bodies in a radical new way, as *enspirited flesh*. We will experience that same wholeness of being that Jesus manifested after his own transformation. Alleluia!

TEACHING TIPS

Oldie But Goodie

Easter is about proclaiming the Good News. Involve the students in writing Easter messages proclaiming the Good News that Jesus has conquered death for everyone. They may wish to use Scripture passages for this. Attach these messages to helium balloons. Include the name and address of the school and instructions to "contact the school if found." As part of an Easter-season prayer service, go outside and release the balloons. Allow a few weeks to see if anyone finds the balloons and responds.

In this context, discuss these two questions with the class:

1. To what degree does each of us really have the responsibility to share the Good News with others?

2. What are some more practical and effective ways students this age could actually fulfill this responsibility?

New Year's Resolutions

In a sense, Easter can be considered the new beginning of our faith each year.

Presuming you talk about Lent in terms of a call to conversion and repentance, it is a good idea to suggest that the students make one *meaningful* and *realistic* Easter resolution aimed at giving new life to their faith during the Easter season.

Discuss realistic resolutions together.

During the last class before Easter, ask the students to write down one Easter resolution, seal them in envelopes you provide, and write their names on the outside. Collect these, possibly in the context of a short penance service around the theme of Good Friday.

A few weeks after Easter, return the envelopes to the students. Ask them to read them and make adjustments to their original resolutions if they feel they want to. Collect them again, providing glue or new envelopes so they can reseal them.

Sometime during the summer, mail these to the students inside another envelope in which you have written a short personal message.

You're a Good Egg

Pass out construction paper. Have each student draw an egg over the full surface of the paper and then print his or her name in the center. Pass out several colorful felt-tip markers to each student. Play the game Musical Eggs. Pass the eggs until the record (of Easter music) stops, then have each student draw a symbol or print a wish or a blessing for the person whose egg he or she has. (Suggest words of hope and life, symbols of new life, joy, and the like.) After several exchanges, collect all the eggs and return them to the individuals whose names are in the center. Have each student reflect on the egg, which is now decorated with messages of the Easter season. Then ask how he or she can break out of the shell to witness to Jesus in joy, hope, and new life. Have the individual answer that question by drawing his or her own symbol or words on the egg. Ask each student to tape his or her egg on a chart or bulletin board. Praise God for his reflection of joy, hope, and new life in each of us. End with singing ''New Hope,'' by Carey Landry, from the album *Hi God II.*

Spring Poetry

Use the pattern for a cinquain or similar verse-form like the haiku to begin a reflection on spring and Easter. Here is an example of a cinquain, which follows this typical pattern:

One-word noun
Two adjectives
Three verb forms
Four-word descriptive phrase
One-word noun (synonym of first noun)

Spring
Fresh, Green
Waking, Sprouting, Reaching
Jesus Invites; He Brings
Life

That Time Again

Involve the students in making Easter cards to send to their parents, to parish shut-ins, to parishioners in nursing homes. Discuss the various themes and meanings of this greatest of feasts in the Church. List these on the board as they are discussed, together with visual symbols associated with the feast. Now help each student write a haiku (see above) or similar ''poem'' on the theme of Easter to be used on the inside of the card. Have the students design the outside with an appropriate picture or symbol. Provide a list of the names and addresses of people to whom the students can send their cards.

You may wish to make this a kind of contest. Have the students help you pick the best card and make this the ''class card.'' For a minimal cost you can make enough copies of it so that each student can have two or three to send to whomever they wish.

'Tis the Season

Assign (or have each student draw from a hat) the name of a child from a lower grade. Provide the students with kite-making materials: strong tissue paper, paste, string, etc. You can get sticks for the frames from most craft shops. The students should decorate their kites with Easter, spring, or summer sayings — for instance, ''Free As the Wind.'' Encourage the students' creativity both in developing the saying and in putting it on the kite in an artistic fashion.

Arrange for the students to give these to the children they were assigned or whom they picked in the draw. Consider having your students help the younger children fly the kites after school on a given day.

Variation: Use the kites as a decoration for a school liturgy before giving them to the younger children.

Year-End Review

On a large piece of poster board or butcher paper, sketch the outline of a tree without leaves. If feasible, have the class make a number of small leaf-shaped pieces of paper in various colors; otherwise provide the "leaves" for the students. Divide the class into groups and assign each group one or more chapters in the textbook. Ask the groups to develop review questions related to their chapter (or chapters) and write these on the leaves, one question to a leaf. Each group receives a fixed number of leaves with which to work.

Collect all the leaves and place them in a box or paper bag. When it is time to review, draw out a leaf, read the question, and call upon a student to attempt to answer it. If the correct answer is given, the student is allowed to paste or pin it on the tree.

If no one can answer it correctly, that question is assigned as homework and the leaf goes back into the bag.

Ask as many questions a day as needed until all the leaves end up on the tree.

Chapter 3
Mary and the Saints

Throughout its history, the Church has always given devotion to Mary and the saints a special place in the faith life of the people. Three basic reasons motivate the Church's treatment of Mary and the saints. They can be summarized by the words honor, edification, and intercession. These three concepts should be the central themes of our own catechesis when we seek to nurture devotion to the saints in our children. Let's briefly review each of them.

Honor. There is a basic human instinct to single out and pay special honor to those in our midst who have provided a special, often heroic service to the community. It is natural for us to honor human greatness. The practice is as old as human nature itself and is clearly evident throughout secular history right up to our own time. We still erect statues and monuments to our heroes and heroines. We name buildings, schools, streets, and parks after them. For some of the most famous, we establish "feast days." If this is common and acceptable in the secular society, it shouldn't be surprising that the Church would do the same for the heroes and heroines within the family of faith.

There is one big difference though, which we need to stress with the children. The achievements the Church recognizes as great aren't always considered so great in secular society. The Church's heroes and heroines usually excelled in virtues like patience, humility, self-sacrifice, humble service to the less fortunate, or dedication to prayer.

In other words, the Church uses a somewhat different measure of greatness than secular society is apt to use. The Church measures greatness in terms of how well a person identifies himself or herself with the convictions and values of Jesus. The Church gives special honor to those who achieved heroic identification with Jesus within the circumstances of their own lives, no matter how humble those circumstances might have been. Genius, fame, wealth, or high position in society doesn't make saints. Faith in and identification with Jesus do. In that light, anyone can become a saint and everyone is called to become a saint. The Church simply honors those of us who have clearly achieved that faith in and identification with Jesus.

Edification. The Church also has a somewhat pragmatic reason for recognizing and honoring the heroes and heroines in our family of faith. By calling attention to them, the Church provides us with powerful examples and encouragement as we strive in our own lives to identify with Jesus and live according to his convictions and values. Unfortunately, today's society has given a somewhat negative connotation to the word *saint*. Often *saint* is equated with words like *nerd, square, sissy, goody-goody*, etc. In our catechesis, then, we need to challenge these negative ideas about striving to emulate the saints in our family of faith. The best way to do this is to present our saints as real people, with strengths and weaknesses just the same as ours. They, too, were children who liked to play more than study, who fought with their brothers and sisters, preferred candy to spinach or green beans. The heroism they achieved was achieved a day at a time. There were failures along the way. In short, *how* we present saints to the children is critical if the example of their lives is going to have the desired edifying effect on the children. Otherwise our teaching about the saints runs the danger of becoming a "turnoff" for the children, especially in the middle and upper grades.

Very early in its history, the Church began to encourage the faithful to pray to those we honor as saints. As the practice of devotion to the saints evolved, it came to play a wholesome, integral role in the life of the faith community. Devotion to saints, properly understood, always enhances rather than interferes with our relationship to Jesus and the Father. And God does answer prayers directed to him through his saints. Nowhere is this more clear than in the Church's devotion to Mary and in the history of her efficacious role as intercessor — beginning with the wedding feast at Cana.

So, we should include in our catechesis about saints a careful explanation of their role as intercessors and an introduction to the various devotions that have earned a solid part in the faith life of the Church.

THEOLOGY UPDATE

Prayer and Intercession

There are two issues we need to consider when we discuss the role of Mary and the saints as intercessors for us before God. The first is the nature and efficacy of prayer in general. Simply stated, "How does prayer work?" The second focuses on the criticism that devotion to saints detracts from or interferes with our relationship to God. Again simply stated, "Why not go directly to God?"

Efficacy of Prayer in General. On the natural level, we can best understand the effect of prayer in terms of relationship. Our relationships with any person, but especially with trusted friends, have the potential to influence us. We can begin to adopt the values, attitudes, interests, and tastes of our friends. Prayer is a way of relating to Mary and the saints, of associating with them and communicating with them. The adage "you are what you think" applies here. If you think about (that is, pray to) Mary or a particular saint, you will begin to take on their qualities and seek to imitate their virtues. Prayer as relationship is clearly efficacious in that sense. But can that form of prayer called prayer of petition "change God's mind"? That is, can we obtain from God favors, help, assistance he had not planned to offer? Those are actually the wrong questions to ask, and they betray a fundamental misconception about the efficacy of prayer. Prayer is not some magic power we can use to manipulate God into doing our will. Prayer of petition, rightly understood, brings our will in line with God's. God already wants all that is good for us and God already knows what is good for us. Jesus' prayer in the Garden of Olives is our model. Like Jesus, we need to pray with confidence, knowing all things are possible to God. But we need to add "not what I will but what you will" (Mark 14:35-36).

Efficacious prayer of petition will have these two qualities: (1) total confidence in God's omnipotence and his love for us; (2) the desire to accept what God judges as good for us, even if it doesn't align with our own limited understanding of what we need at the time.

Saints as Intercessors. But why bother to pray to God through Mary and the saints? Why not pray to God directly? We can, of course, and we should. But in God's economy of salvation, each of us is to help one another experience God and relate to him. In the normal course of things God reveals his presence, his love, his wisdom, and his power through the community, the Church — the communion of saints.

If we can look to our friends on earth to help us experience God's love and help us deepen our own love for God, it stands to reason that our friends who now see God "face to face" can help us even more effectively. To state it another way, God in his wisdom chose to reveal himself to us on earth through the Church, that is, the community of believers with whom we worship, work, and play. Those members of the community whom we now honor as heroes and heroines of faith are still members of the Church, the community of saints. We relate to them through prayer and devotion, just as we truly can relate to our friends on earth.

It's true that at various times in the history of the Church, ignorance caused devotion to the saints to degenerate into superstition bordering on magic if not idolatry. But so did some people's approach to the sacraments degenerate into superstition or magic. That always remains a danger when faith is weak and unlightened. But just as we don't stop celebrating the sacraments because they have sometimes been misunderstood, we don't play down devotion to the saints because there have been excesses and abuses of such devotions at certain times.

The bottom line, then, is this: If we don't hesitate to look to our friends on earth to help us deepen our relationship to God, why should we hesitate to look to our friends in heaven to help us do the same?

This was the understanding of the Church in earliest times. It should continue to be ours today.

TEACHING TIPS

Who Is Mary?

Gather together as many of the traditional pictures of Mary that you can. We want the pictures to speak to the students, so frescoes and mosaics are excellent because the viewer can read into them what he or she wants. When you have gathered these together, ask the students two questions:
- What three feelings or emotions is each picture depicting?
- Which one is your favorite and why?

Obviously, there are no right answers to this little exercise.

Mantra

A mantra is an Eastern form of prayer that allows the pray-er to quiet himself or herself and focus on the interior speaking of the Spirit. A mantra can be a three-, five-, or seven-word phrase that is repeated over and over as one breathes in deeply and exhales quietly. A mantra seeks to soothe the person and relax the mind without making one sleepy. The litanies begun in the Middle Ages were started for much the same reason. Teach the children to sit in as relaxed a position as possible, feet flat on the floor, hands quietly in laps and eyes shut. As the adult, explain that you will be praying the litany with them and their responses will consist of the phrase "Pray for us." Once the students are relaxed, pray the litany with them.

Mary from Scripture

Using the pictures suggested in "Who Is Mary?" (above) or any others collected, have the students title each one from a line from Scripture. Suggest to the students that they use Chapters 1 and 2 of Luke, and John 2 and 19:25-27. This might be done in groups of two or three with each student defending why he or she chose a particular quote.

Ark of the Covenant

One of the favorite images of Mary is that of "ark of the covenant." Have the students read Exodus 25:10-22 and list the contents. Explain that the role of the ark for the people of the Old Testament was the presence of God among them. Why would Mary be referred to as the ark of the covenant? She, too, held the Bread of Life, the New Law, and the King of Israel (symbolized by Aaron's rod).

Mary Is for Today

One of the bigger temptations when talking about Mary is to leave her in her long flowing robes in the first century, or perhaps we might bring her at least into the Middle Ages through the various arts that depict her so well. Our challenge is to have her alive and well for the coming years. Ask the students to go through the local newspaper and cut out two or three articles of interest. In groups of two or three, have them prepare a short commentary on "what Mary's reaction to this would be."

Many Symbols

The Church has symbolized Mary in many ways: *queen* of heaven, *seat* of wisdom, morning *star*, mystical *rose*; most of these names are drawn from scriptural references that have been applied to Mary. Challenge the students to come up with new and contemporary symbols and be ready to explain their meanings.

'Poor People' Rosaries

Have the children make rosaries "for the poor" by tying knots in a long piece of string. They can use the ring from the top of a soft drink can to join the first and fifth decades. A cross can be made with Popsicle sticks and glue. They can color the "beads" with markers.

Have the students use these rosaries during October and/or May if you pray a portion of the rosary during class.

Theology Made Easy

The fifteen mysteries of the rosary are actually a short course in salvation history. When the rosary first became popular, that was one of its purposes: an aid to teach and to help simple folk meditate on the mysteries of salvation. Try this.

- Divide the class into small groups of two or three.
- Assign each group one mystery of the rosary.
- Groups are to do three things: (1) Prepare a short explanation of the mystery assigned to them. (2) On poster paper draw a design, symbol, or picture depicting the central idea or event of the mystery. (3) Find and write on the poster a Scripture passage that deals with the mystery. For the mystery of the Assumption into Heaven and Coronation of Mary there is no direct Scripture reference, but suitable passages can be found in Psalms and in the Apocalypse.
- Have the groups then present their work to the class. Afterward, hang posters around the room or in one of the school corridors.

A Decade a Day

During October and/or May, it is a good practice to say a decade of the rosary each day at the beginning or ending of class. If you do the project described above, use the poster and its Scripture passage as a means of focusing attention on the mystery of the day. In this way you can pray all fifteen decades within the month. Take a little time to discuss the meaning of the mystery before you begin.

Research and Litany

A good project for helping students become better acquainted with Mary is this:

1. Assign each student one or more of the titles of Mary found in her litany. (**Variation:** Form groups and assign each group several titles.)

2. Have the students research Marian titles and try to find references to them in the Old or New Testament and in Church history.

3. Have the students then give reports on their research and attempt to explain the significance of the title in relation to one or another of Mary's attributes or her role in salvation history. For example: House of God = Temple = place where Jesus dwelt.

Some Variations: You could do similar research projects using either the various feasts of Mary and/or her major confirmed apparitions: Fátima, Guadalupe, Lourdes. Have the students do research on the history of the feast or apparition, the shrines, statues, and pictures related to the feast or apparition, and its significance for the life of the Church and the faithful. This could be a rather ambitious project, so give precise instructions on what it is you want the students to do. Suggest resources available to them in the school or local library. Have the students share the reports when they complete them.

Drow Rabclesm (Word Scramble)

A fun filler activity and review activity is the following:

1. Give each student a slip of paper with one of Mary's titles taken from the litany. (As a variation, substitute a mystery of the rosary or a feast of Mary for one of her titles.)

2. Each student then turns the word or phrase into a Word Scramble.

3. Call on one student to put his or her Word Scramble on the board.

4. Have the other students guess what the word is. The first to get it correct puts his or her word on the board. Repeat as often as desired.

Variation: Do the same activity, but divide the class into teams. Keep track of how many guesses it takes for a team to guess its word when it takes its turn. The team with the lowest score at the end wins.

This activity can be used with virtually any topic. The only rule is to restrict students to a definite topic. For example, all words must be taken from the Nicene Creed or a Scripture passage.

Every Day Is Mother's Day

A fun art project is to have the students design and then make a Mother's Day card for Mary. They should include some verse or suitable statement on the inside. Stress that they should reflect Mary's real role in their lives, not just sentiment. Use the finished projects to decorate the bulletin board, Bible shrine, or if you have one, a Marian shrine.

Modern Madonnas

Begin by discussing with the students various aspects of Mary's life and her role in Salvation History — in keeping with the students' level of understanding (for example, Mary's faith-filled "yes" at the Annunciation, Mary's marriage to Joseph, Mary as a proud and caring mother, Mary as a loving wife and housekeeper, Mary as a disciple, Mary as a widow, Mary as a witness to her Son's death, and Mary as the Queen of Heaven).

Now invite the students to make "holy pictures" in which they use pictures of women in real-life situations (from magazines, newspapers, etc.) to represent Mary in one or another of these ways. They should give their holy pictures appropriate titles. Use colored construction paper to mount the holy pictures. Display the finished products around the room. The activity helps students realize that Mary is a real person who lived an ordinary life in many respects despite her unique role in history.

Feasts of Mary

Below is a list of the major feasts or optional memorials of Mary currently celebrated in the United States. Assign a feast to each individual student or group of students. (You may not wish to use all the feasts or memorials.) They are to "research" and prepare a report on the feast assigned them. Reports can be oral, in the form of a collage, a mobile, a poem, or other imaginative work.

The old daily missals usually gave a good history or explanation of each of these feasts. If you can locate a few of these, they would make a good resource for the children to use.

The feasts or optional memorials are:
* January 1 — Solemnity of Mary, Mother of God.
* February 2 — Presentation of the Lord.
* February 11 — Our Lady of Lourdes.
* March 25 — Annunciation of the Lord.
* May 31 — Visitation of the Blessed Virgin Mary.
* July 16 — Our Lady of Mount Carmel.
* August 15 — Assumption of the Blessed Virgin Mary.
* August 22 — Queenship of Mary.
* September 8 — Birth of Mary.
* September 15 — Our Lady of Sorrows.
* October 7 — Our Lady of the Rosary.
* November 21 — Presentation of the Blessed Virgin Mary.
* December 8 — Immaculate Conception of the Blessed Virgin Mary.

• December 25 — Christmas (birth of the Lord).

You may wish to have all the reports completed in connection with a particular lesson or unit. Or you may prefer to spread the reports out through the year. Artistic reports such as a collage should be presented in a "show and tell" manner. Oral reports and poems can be recited to the class.

Sing to Mary

Our tradition abounds with hymns devoted to Mary. Here, our interest is not so much with music as with the lyrics. Gather current and older hymnals. Assign the students a specific topic related to Mary: her Immaculate Conception, her faith, her motherhood, her suffering, etc. Have them look through the hymnals and choose a song whose lyrics deal with the topic.

Now discuss the hymn and have the students rate it from 1 to 5 (5 = good theology; 1 = poor theology). This is an interesting way to help the students move from sentimental to solid devotion to Mary, rooted in a good understanding of her special qualities and deeds.

Variation: Pick out ahead of time what you consider some of the better, theologically solid hymns devoted to Mary. They may deal with a particular quality or they may praise Mary in a more global way. Share and analyze the lyrics with the children, using the hymn as the content of the "lesson." The poetic and imaginative quality of the lyrics can help younger children grasp the theological concepts more easily. If you have any musical talent, also teach the children how to sing the hymn and use it as a prayer to close the class.

Mary in Scripture

Apart from the Christmas narratives found in Matthew (Chapters 1 and 2) and Luke (Chapter 2), Mary is not mentioned a great deal in the New Testament. Here, as a quick reference, are the other major incidents where Mary is mentioned:

• Annunciation and Visitation (Luke 1:26-55).
• Presentation in the Temple. Simeon's prediction (Luke 2:22-35).
• Finding Jesus in the Temple (Luke 2:41-51).
• Wedding at Cana (John 2:1-11).
• Discipleship of Mary (Luke 8:19-21 and 11:27-28).
• Mary at the Cross of Jesus (John 19:25-28).
• Mary with the Apostles at Pentecost (Acts 1:13-14).

There are also a number of Old Testament passages applied to Mary as prophetic foreshadowings, but most are applied only in an indirect way. Yet, these few references have been the subjects of a great volume of Christian art and are the basis of the theological reflection of the Church for twenty centuries. Throughout the year, bring in various examples of masterpieces based on one or another of these Scripture passages. Use these masterpieces as a way to introduce the different dimensions of Mary's role in the Church.

The Bells of St. Mary

Most dioceses have a number of parishes named after Mary. They often go simply by the name, "St. Mary's," but in fact have often been dedicated to Mary under a more complete title, like St. Mary of the Seven Sorrows or St. Mary, Seat of Wisdom. It might make a good project for older students to gather pictures of each St. Mary's church in the diocese, together with its complete title. These could then be formed into a bulletin-board display by the students in relation to one of Mary's feast days. It could be titled "St. Mary in Our Diocese."

Teach the Classics

A number of Marian prayers can be considered classics in the Church, among them the Angelus and the Hail, Holy Queen. During the course of the year take the time to teach the students the hymns you feel appropriate for their age-group. You can introduce a different prayer every few weeks. Before having the students memorize the prayer, however, take time in class to analyze it. Comment on it phrase by phrase, expanding on various titles used, the significance of the petitions, and so forth. Once you have introduced a new prayer, use it to begin or end the class several times in a row to help the children learn it.

As you have probably done with prayers like the Our Father, consider helping the children put gestures with the prayer so that it can be prayed and "acted out" at the same time.

Make It Personal

Mary has so many titles and there are so many facets to her role in the Church that it can be confusing to children. Try this.

Using Mary's Litany, list on the board as many titles as you feel appropriate. Discuss each of these to ensure that the children understand the title's significance.

Now invite the children to "adopt" one title that seems to have special meaning to them — for instance, Virgin Most Faithful, Queen of Peace, or Tower of Ivory. Encourage them to use it as their "personal" way to address Mary when they pray to her. In a *reverent* sense it can be their special "nickname" for Mary, just as they probably use special "nicknames" of endearment in their family for themselves and for their own parents. This helps make their prayer to Mary more personal.

'Baseball Card Saints'

Ask the students to give you the names of saints they have heard about and would like to study. Examples: Nicholas, Valentine, Francis of Assisi, Anthony, Patrick, and Bernadette. List these on the board.

Add to this list names they may not be familiar with: the patron and co-patrons of Europe (Boniface; Cyril and Methodius), the patron of students (Thomas Aquinas), etc. Add "American" saints such as Isaac Jogues, Elizabeth Seton, Kateri Tekakwitha, and Mother Cabrini.

Also, consider saints that have a special interest to youth: Don Bosco, Maria Goretti, Dominic Savio, Thérèse of Lisieux, Maximilian Kolbe, etc. Don't forget founders of religious communities like Benedict, Dominic, Ignatius of Loyola, Vincent de Paul, John Baptist de La Salle, and Teresa of Ávila.

After compiling a suitable list, divide it up, assigning one or more saints to each student. Have the students then make baseball-type cards on each of the saints assigned to them. Use 5" x 7" cards. On one side they should compile the following information:

Name:_____

Dates of birth/death:_____

Feast day:_____

Deeds for which the saint is noted and other facts of interest:_____
_____
_____

On the back side of the card, have the students draw a design, print a key word, or in other ways decorate the card to depict a quality or deed of the saint.

For example: St. Thérèse of Lisieux: *flower*; St. Francis of Assisi: *birds*.

To help the students during this project, you will need to provide one or more of the following resources from the school or local library:

√ *A Saint for Your Name (Boys)* and *A Saint for Your Name (Girls)*, Our Sunday Visitor.

√ Butler's *Lives of the Saints* (four volumes).

√ *Saints of the Day*, Leonard Foley, St. Anthony Press.

√ *A Dictionary of Saints*, Donald Attwater, Penguin Books.

√ *Maryknoll Catholic Dictionary* (Appendix III contains a list of all patron saints of professions and occupations and their feasts; Appendix VI lists patrons of countries; Appendix IX gives a list of most saints' names and feast days).

√ *Catholic Encyclopedia.*

Using the Cards

Here are a few ways to study the information gathered on the cards.

1. *Card Swap:* Devote a class to a card swap. Have the students trade a card with a classmate, study the information on it, and then trade for another. Continue until every student has had the chance to trade at least five or more times.

Collect all cards. Draw one and ask who can tell you about this saint. Usually three or four students can tell you something about the saint whose card you have drawn. Continue as time permits.

2. *Class Calendar:* On a large piece of poster board, design a calendar of the twelve months of the year. Go through the calendar

month by month asking the students to give you the feast day of any saint they have whose feast falls on a day of that month. When the saints on all the cards have their feasts posted on the calendar, place it in a prominent place in the classroom. Refer to it regularly, calling on that saint in your class prayer on his or her feast day. Review that saint's card on that day.

3. *Bingo:* With student help, make bingo cards. In each square, put the name of a saint you have studied on the "baseball cards." Bingo cards don't have to be the same. When you have enough bingo cards for each group of two or three students to have one, draw out a "baseball card" from the the pile and read one or more clues. For example: This saint is a patron of _____ .

This saint was born in _____ and founded _____ community. Have the various groups cover the names as in bingo. When they have a row covered they can call out. Check to see that you described the saints they covered.

4. *Crossword Puzzles:* Form small groups. Give each group eight to ten "baseball cards," then have the groups make crossword puzzles. Clues are taken from the cards. Saints' names are arranged in "crossword" fashion as the answers to the clues. When the puzzles are complete, have the groups trade with one another to see who can solve the other's puzzle the fastest.

5. *File box:* When you are finished using the cards in one or more of the ways suggested, put together a file box of these cards in alphabetical order. Use as a reference throughout the year for the other projects.

Stained-Glass Windows

Have the students do research as described in the "baseball cards" for their name saint. Then have each student design and make a "stained-glass window" in honor of his or her saint. Encourage creativity by providing colored cellophane paper or colored construction paper, etc.

Display the completed windows around the classroom, in halls around the school, or in the back of the church on the Feast of All Saints.

That Person Was a Saint

Instruct the students to ask their parents to describe to them some member of the family (grandparent, uncle, brother, or sister) whom parents feel was a very special person and who possessed qualities you usually ascribe to saints. It may also be an acquaintance: a former teacher, pastor, neighbor, or friend.

With a parent's help, have each student prepare a brief report on that person, his or her lifestyle, and the saintly qualities he or she possessed. Then have the students give the reports. Summarize the session by emphasizing that saints are all around us, not just in storybooks. Note some of the qualities or deeds that are within range of the students' own experience.

Litany of Saints — A Day at a Time

During the month of November begin each class by praying a portion of the Litany of Saints. Research one or more of the saints mentioned in the portion prayed that day and share it with the students.

Dress-Up Day

Intermediate-grade children can be asked, with parental help, to prepare a costume of a particular saint assigned to them. (It is amazing what can be done with bathrobes, dishtowels, and cardboard.) They can wear their costume in a procession at the All Saints' Day Mass or in a "dress-up day" related to the feast — for example, Halloween.

Saints Today

Review various saints from the past: the virtues they displayed, the kinds of people they helped, the trials they experienced, the deeds for which they are famous. On the board, compile a list of common traits, experiences, etc. With the students' help, now list on the board various occupations today that interest them: professional athlete, rock star, astronaut; add others like teacher, parent, doctor, carpenter, and bus driver. Assign one of these occupations to each student.

Have the students make up a "life of the saint" for a fictitious person in that occupation in our day. What virtues would the saint display? Whom would the saint help? What problems might the saint encounter? What deeds would the saint achieve?

Have the students write up and share their stories. Summarize by stressing that it is possible to be a saint today as in the past. Observe that the kinds of virtues needed tend to remain the same in every age, but the specific deeds may change.

Pen Pals

Assign each student a saint or let the students pick their own. Instruct them to write a letter to their saint asking for advice related to a real or fictitious problem young people their age commonly experience: getting along with a younger brother or sister, trouble with a school subject, a particular fear, peer pressure, etc. Collect the letters and place them in a box. Next, have the students draw out a letter (replacing it if they get their own) and then proceed to answer it as if they were that saint to whom it was addressed. Ask the students to share the results.

Summarize by stressing that we should not hesitate to bring our real problems to our saint-friend through prayer. The saints are interested in us. They can and will help us if we ask their advice.

Let Us Pray

Using a missal or missalettes, have the students look up examples of the various orations (prayers) used in the liturgy of different saints' feasts.

After they get a feel for the style, direct each student to compose an oration for the saint of his or her choice, such as the student's name saint.

These can be printed on small cards to be used as bookmarks.

Feast-Day Cards

On a small card have each student put his or her own name, the name of his or her patron saint, and that saint's feast day. Collect the cards and redistribute them so that each student has another student's card.

Now ask the students to design a feast-day card for the person whose name they have drawn. Collect these and present them to the students on their "feast day."

Parish Saints

Tour the parish church, having the students note every saint who is any way represented there: in stained-glass windows, statues, paintings, murals, frescoes, etc. This can be especially fruitful in older churches.

Divide the students into groups, assigning one saint to each group. Have the groups prepare a short biography of their saint. Arrange to have a different biography printed in the parish bulletin each week for the next several weeks.

Chapter 4
Spirituality and Prayer

We don't often think in terms of developing a spirituality in children when we are engaged in religious education. Spirituality seems so grown-up, more appropriate for adults. The fact is we can lay solid foundations and begin to nurture a spirituality in children at a very early age. Religious education classes can be an effective vehicle for doing so. Let's review some key ideas about the nature of spirituality and the possible implications these have for our catechetical ministry.

A good working definition of spirituality that is both simple and sufficiently comprehensive is this: one's personal relationship with God. A spiritual life is no more and no less than that. To begin, then, let's explain what we mean by personal. A spiritual life will flow from and reflect our own personality traits. For example, some of us are by nature more passive, reflective, less inclined to displays of emotion, less in need of external stimulation. Others of us are the opposite. We take a more active role, express emotion freely, thrive on external stimulation and become easily bored without it. Our basic personality traits will to a large extent determine what will most effectively assist us in both experiencing and responding to God's presence in our life. In other words, our personality determines the kind of spirituality and the kind of spiritual practices most appropriate for us.

For example, we talk about a Franciscan spirituality, a Sulpician spirituality, a Dominican spirituality. Insofar as each of these is different (all have certain common characteristics), they reflect the personalities of the persons after whom they are named. People attracted to a particular spirituality usually have certain personality traits that are similar. The style, the kinds of ascetic practices, the method of prayer of a particular spirituality will have a certain "natural" feel to those people who are attracted to it. They feel "at home" with that overall manner of relating to God.

Several practical implications are suggested when we say one's spiritual life should reflect one's personality. First, we must be careful not to impose our own particular style of spirituality on our children. Those who have personality traits similar to ours may find our spirituality appropriate, but each child is different. Our style of prayer, for example, could be all wrong for some children who have personalities quite different from our own. In teaching prayer forms and in providing prayer services, then, strive to offer a variety of approaches. Second, and more important, we should help our children discover the manner of relating to God that is most natural for them. Assure them that there are many ways to pray, to experience God, to discover God's will, and to respond to God. What works for one person may not work for another. It's okay, for example, if they don't enjoy a particular style of praying or a particular setting for prayer. The important thing is that they do form a personal relationship with God suited to their own gifts and limits.

Now a word about the concept of relationship in this context of spirituality. Any authentic relationship is dynamic. It cannot stay exactly the same very long. It either continues to deepen or it weakens. An authentic relationship is existential. It focuses on the present even though it has roots in the past and anticipates a future. This focusing on the "here and now" helps it maintain its dynamic character. An authentic relationship is dialogic. That is, it is sustained by an ongoing two-way communication. It involves sensitivity and listening. It involves openness and honesty in sharing oneself.

The spiritual life is relational — a dynamic, existential, dialogical relationship with God. To help our children lay the foundations for this kind of relationship with God in their lives, we need to do several things. We need to emphasize and illustrate that a relationship with God is anything but dull and boring. It is full of surprises and challenges. It is often like a game of "hide and seek." Sometimes God hides and we must seek him out. Other times we prefer to hide, but God ultimately tracks us down. Though rituals and formula prayers should play a role in our relationship with God, the spiritual life as such is not ritual and formula. It is dynamic. It is exciting. At peak moments it will be filled with passion and the keenest emotions. At other times it can be steeped in sorrow and discouragement. But it is not boring. In ways appropriate to the age-group, present this dynamic aspect of the spiritual life.

Stress, too, that we should strive to relate to God as we are, and not in some artificial way. God is as interested in our day-to-day adventures, successes, and failures as we are. What is important to us just now is also important to him. God is interested in the things children like: basketball, dolls, dirt bikes and skate boards, for example. And God is concerned about the challenges or difficulties children face, such as tests, cranky parents, and homework. In other words, assure the children that God is interested in them right now, precisely as children, and wants to be invited into their children's world. There will be time enough for them to adopt more adult concerns and priorities when they are adults.

Finally, by teaching specific prayer techniques appropriate to the age-group, we nurture in our children the skills of sensitivity and openness to God's presence in their lives — in sacrament, Scripture, community, and nature. Though God is by nature invisible, he is anything but distant if we know how to look for him. Whatever you do to nurture in children a sense of God's continuing presence in daily life — and a sensitivity to how he reveals himself — is foundational to spiritual life.

Catechesis has been defined as "teaching the art of reading the signs by which God reveals himself and fostering the desire to respond to God thus revealed." To the degree that our catechesis teaches that art and fosters that desire in our children, we are playing an essential role in developing their spiritual life — their own personal relationship to God — no matter what age they are.

THEOLOGY UPDATE

Spiritual Renaissance

In the last several years, there has been a virtual renaissance of interest in the spiritual life. There are several possible causes for this. Many people have become disenchanted with the ephemeral, materialistic values that permeate much of our society. They are searching for more depth and substance than can be obtained in the *National Enquirer*, on TV, or in shopping malls. Also, in our fast-changing, often confusing, and potentially volatile times, many people are seeking stability and peace by turning to God.

Ultimately, however, we can trace the source of this renaissance directly to the Spirit of God, whose presence and energy has been keenly experienced in the Church since Vatican Council II. For a period immediately after the council, it appeared anything but a spiritual renaissance was taking place. Interest in traditional devotions and prayer forms waned rapidly. The value of traditional ascetical practices like fasting was challenged. Religious communities sometimes abandoned a more contemplative lifestyle and redirected their energies to ministries of a more active, seemingly secular nature. Much attention was given to the human sciences like psychology and psychotherapy. A new generation of Catholics began to emerge who were more familiar with Jung and Frankl than they were with Teresa of Ávila or Francis de Sales. Liturgical celebrations focused more on active participation than on quiet reflection.

Looking back, we can now see this was a necessary phase of renewal, not renewal itself. Essential spiritual values and practices had to first be purged, as it were, of centuries of culturally accrued half-truths before they could be rediscovered in their purity and properly adapted by the Church to meet the needs of the people in our post-industrial society. As the smoke first generated by the Vatican II renewal begins to clear, what we see is a more holistic and balanced spirituality emerging, one clearly suited to the needs of today's Christians. Several characteristics mark this renewed spirituality present in the Church today.

First, spirituality is now drawing its strength and guidance from the very origins of Christianity, namely, Jesus and the Scriptures. Modern Scripture scholarship has helped us rediscover our true roots and reclaim the simple but profound vision Jesus first proclaimed. We are rediscovering the scriptural meaning and value of practices such as fasting. The biblical concept of community and the value of communal prayer have become more central to our personal spiritual life. The fruit of prayer is seen more in terms of effecting works of justice and peace than in terms of "acquiring grace" or "saving our soul."

Second, the valid and therefore useful discoveries in the human sciences are now being integrated in a more balanced way into our spiritual life. It is interesting to note that much of what these sciences (depth psychology and psychotherapy, for instance) can tell us actually vindicates rather than repudiates the insights, practices, and experiences of the great spiritual masters of our tradition — the Desert Fathers, Teresa of Ávila, Ignatius of Loyola, and so forth. Consequently, more and more people are returning to the works of these great masters. But they are now reading them with a new awareness and appreciation provided by knowledge of the human sciences.

Third, in our more ecumenical and multicultural era, our spiritual life is also now being enriched by knowledge of other traditions and other religions. Most obvious is the influence that Eastern religions are having on our own spirituality. Many people now combine the physical discipline of Yoga, for example, with their routine of meditation and asceticism. The holistic and more detached understanding of the material universe that permeates Eastern religions is providing a wholesome counterpoint to those of us in the Western world who are prone to worship technology and compartmentalize reality. Contemporary spiritual giants of our own culture, like Thomas Merton, pioneered this rapprochement between Eastern and Western spiritualities.

Fourth, there has been a renewal of our understanding of liturgy as the official spiritual life of the Church. Personal spirituality today is drawing more of its energy from involvement in the liturgical life of the Church. At the same time, the deepening of personal spirituality within the community is providing a new vitality to our communal celebrations.

Next, traditional practices of the pre-Vatican era — like regular meditation, praying the Divine Office alone or communally, fasting, devotion to Mary and the saints — are gradually being reintroduced into our spiritual life. Having been purged of various superstitions and pietistic sentiments — where necessary — they are once again being seen as valid means for cultivating the spiritual life.

In all of this, one thing is clear: "We can't go back home." Those who nostalgically long for the "good old days" will be disappointed. Spirituality in the Church is marked by pluralism, and it is taking on a distinctly lay-oriented quality. Monastic spirituality, that was simply imitated by the laity in a less perfect way, had dominated the spiritual life of the Church prior to Vatican II. There was a sameness about the spiritual life throughout the Church. This is not true today. Spirituality is coming out of the cloister and being reborn in the kitchen and on the freeway. In the process, a rich diversity of practices is evolving as people adapt their spiritual life to their particular circumstances and their personal gifts. Spiritual directors are in great demand. Discernment of the Spirit in one's personal journey is given much more importance.

Some are scandalized by this diversity, regard these movements as dangerous novelties, and cling tenaciously to more traditional rituals and devotions. There are, in fact, some fringe movements today that are suspect. They border on the bizarre and tend to attract less emotionally stable personalities. However, these are not a threat to the Church so much as they are a threat to vulnerable individuals.

In summary, an authentic renaissance in spirituality is taking place. It is scriptural; it integrates the past masters with contemporary insights into human nature; it is more ecumenical and multicultural; it is liturgical; it reclaims the authentic practices from our tradition; it is more lay-oriented and pluralistic. In short, the spiritual life in the Church is alive and well — thanks to the Spirit.

TEACHING TIPS

Best Friends

To help the students see spirituality as developing and maintaining a personal relationship with God, try this. List or invite the students to help you list several essential characteristics of friendship — for example, sharing time, sharing secrets, being loyal, and doing little favors.

When you've developed a representative list for this age-group, make this point: "Jesus wants to be best friends with you. Being Christian means being 'best friends' with Jesus."

Now ask the students if they can think of any concrete ways they feel Jesus is showing his friendship. Some possible suggestions: he's loyal, always there in the Eucharist or in prayer, ready to help. Next, ask the students if they can think of one concrete way they could act more like a friend to Jesus at this time in their life. List their suggestions on the board.

Finally, encourage the students to pick out one practice they are willing to carry out this week that could make their friendship with Jesus more real. Explain that in their effort to actually do it, they are developing their spiritual life.

Repeat this periodically, asking the students to think of and pursue one special act of friendship toward Jesus that week.

God Is . . .

To help the students relate to God in a more personal way, suitable to their own personal needs and temperament, list on a worksheet the following qualities (and feel free to add others):

Instruct the students to mark any three qualities that best describe what they like most about God.

Since many of these aren't the "traditional" words we use when describing God, assure them that God really does have these kinds of qualities — and many, many more.

Next, invite the students to share what they marked and explain, as best they can, why they like these qualities of God. Finally, encourage them to include these thoughts about God in their prayer-conversations with him. This will help them experience God as real, and as a personal friend, rather than as a vague "force somewhere out there."

You can extend this exercise by providing a second worksheet with the same or similar list of qualities on it. This time, have the students mark down the three qualities they feel God finds most attractive about them.

Both exercises can help students this age begin to picture God in ways they can relate to.

Simon of Cyrene

Discuss with the students how different people have "crosses" to bear, much like Jesus. Give some examples and ask the student to come up with some of their own, based on people they actually know (they don't have to give actual names). For example, a mother who has a retarded child that demands all her attention, an elderly person afflicted with arthritis, a family with the father out of work.

Share the story of how Simon was asked to help Jesus carry his Cross. Ask the students to identify one person they know who is "carrying a cross." During Lent, they should then decide on some *tactful* way to help that person, even for a little while, to "carry that cross" (for instance, volunteering to baby-sit for the mother of the retarded child).

Encourage the students to start right in their own home, if possible, by identifying some "cross" a family member may be experiencing and then finding a way to make it a little easier for that person to carry his or her cross.

Handing on the Faith

Because of their relationship with their grandparents, children usually respect and relate well with our senior citizens. Ask some of your older parishioners to talk to the children about prayer customs and traditions they learned in their youth, many of which are still valid today. For example, novenas, the Way of the Cross, various devotions to Mary and the saints, forty hours devotions, rogation days, and family prayer customs. This helps our Catholic heritage come alive for the children.

What's in a Name?

The word "God" tends to be very vague for children. Ask them to play this game with you for six weeks: "We will not use the word 'God' in class without adding the phrase Our Father or Our Brother or Holy Spirit." This helps personalize their concept of God, and also makes praying more personal.

When to Pray

It is not always best to start a session with prayer. Rather, interject a spontaneous prayer or call for the students to pray at various times during the session. Many opportunities will present themselves; for example, when you hear of a sick parent, stop and pray for the parent and all sick people. At an appropriate time, pause to look out the window, then ask all to thank God our Father for his gifts in nature. (A word of caution: If you are not personally comfortable with this form of praying, it is best not to use it. Children will pick up that feeling.)

Prayer from Around the World

Use the natural curiosity children have to introduce different forms of prayer. Initially this can be done at the factual level. For example, Muslims stop to pray six times a day. Some Eastern religions put emphasis on body posture and breath control (Yoga). Psalm prayers of the Hebrews are chanted. At the next level you can ask the students to experiment with one or another of these prayer forms. It adds a new dimension to their prayer life and also helps emphasize that "everyone prays."

'Dear Diary . . .'

Children love diaries. Each child could be given a notebook and guided in simple journal-keeping. The entries, three or four times a week, would begin by saying a simple phrase such as "Dear Jesus" or "God my Friend," and then the daily events relayed. When this becomes routine, the catechist can suggest entries on various topics: how I feel about my parents, the loneliness of the elderly, Jesus as gift of himself in the Eucharist, and so forth.

An Easy Formula

Paragraph 113 of *Sharing the Light of Faith: National Catechetical Directory for Catholics of the United States* directs us in our catechesis to prepare our students for liturgy. All liturgical prayer falls easily into this format: (1) *greeting* — "God our Father. . ."; (2) *remember* — "as you promised. . ."; (3) *request* — "please help. . ."; (4) *praise* — "you can do this because you are so good. . . ." Students using that formula to compose a prayer for the classroom and home will have no reason to wonder if it is a "good" prayer.

Memorizing

To avoid the boredom of memorization, try this. Ask the students to develop an appropriate "rubric" for the various phrases of the prayer: arm and hand gestures, body positions, etc. Some of the more expressive signs used by the deaf can be used effectively here. This activity helps the students think through the meaning of the phrases of each prayer.

Prefaces as Prayers

There are over eighty seasonal and special occasion prefaces contained in the Sacramentary. Any number of these can be prayed "as is" or easily adapted for use as opening prayers in classes. The students can recite or sing the "Holy, Holy, Holy" in response. Since prefaces always contain an excellent theological summary of the season or occasion, they can also be discussed by the students for that purpose.

Praying Through the Eyes of Others

Sometimes students are self-conscious when asked to compose a prayer or to pray spontaneously expressing their own feelings. A good way to help them overcome this is to provide each student with a short news article taken from current newspapers or newsmagazines. Articles should deal with various life situations: accident victim, success story, initiation of an important project, racial incident, etc. Ask the students to compose the kind of prayer the person (or persons) in their article might say in that situation. They will find this less threatening, but they are also learning two important lessons: (1) how to make up a prayer and (2) why prayer is appropriate in all life situations.

Liturgical Seasons

Children like to become acquainted with the liturgical seasons. Use a factual approach, asking them to research the key themes, important Scripture passages, liturgical symbols, liturgical colors, traditional hymns and customs associated with each season. Different groups could be assigned different seasons and can present results as a project.

How Others Pray

This project helps children discover that prayer is important to more people than their religion teachers. Ask each student to conduct a poll of about eight adults, including their parent (or parents). Help them compose the questions that would deal with these topics:

- When do you pray?
- What form does your prayer most often take?
- Who do you usually pray to — God the Father? Jesus? The Holy Spirit? A saint?
- How did you feel about praying when in junior high?
- What do you find helps you the most?
- What is your biggest problem in praying?

The results of these polls can be shared and tabulated.

Mass Next Sunday

All prayer culminates in the Sunday liturgy. To help the students approach this celebration more prayerfully:

1. Have them find the common thread that binds the Sunday readings together, and choose a theme for a homily.

2. Take one or two of the prayers in the liturgy and ask the students to rewrite them, explaining them or their meaning to the other students.

Chapter 5
Liturgy and Sacraments

We can get some helpful insights into the teaching of liturgy by taking a good look at the nature of liturgy itself, be it the various celebrations of the Eucharist or any other sacrament.

First, liturgy is highly experiential. Liturgy is *action*. It is rooted in the actions of Jesus. It is also highly *sensate*. It utilizes things we can see, hear, touch and feel, even smell and taste. Good liturgy bombards our senses.

Liturgy is celebration. It is intended to affect our mood and our emotions. Also, the mood and emotions we bring to liturgical celebrations will have an influence on the celebrations, whether we intend it or not.

Finally, liturgy is also referred to as the "sacred mysteries." There is something mysterious about liturgy, even in the popular meaning of that word. Things happen "behind the scenes." Familiar objects like water, oil, bread, and wine — even candles, flowers, and gestures — take on new meanings and hint of unseen realities.

All this suggests that liturgy is first of all intended to be experienced, and reflected upon, primarily, after the fact. We can compare it to good art forms. In a real sense good liturgy is itself an art form.

Even the uninitiated can enjoy and appreciate a ballet or an opera. Persons trained in the art forms may more fully appreciate them and notice the nuances of the artists. But everyone can get caught up in the music, the graceful movements, the costumes and sets. The response of the audience can give the uninitiated clues as to the significance of what is taking place. Good art touches the human spirit directly, by its own power and authenticity. It does not depend upon knowledge of the artist or the history of the art form. As the saying goes, "Art just is."

Liturgy "just is" also. It can touch the human spirit directly, affect us, grace us. Probably all of us have, at least once, had a non-Catholic friend remark to us how moved and impressed he or she was by having attended one of our elaborate liturgies. The vestments, the solemn movements, the incense, and the music evoked feelings of reverence and awe in the person even though he or she totally lacked the theological understanding of the event.

As our children grow they should be educated formally in liturgy. They need to learn about the scriptural roots of our liturgy. They need to know the nature of and traditions behind the signs, symbols, and rituals most commonly employed in liturgy. They need to grasp the theology of sacraments and the role of sacraments in the faith life of the community.

But let's not be in too big a hurry. Most people would much rather attend a good play than take a course in the history of the drama. Too much theory and not enough experience of liturgy can rob the liturgy of its power to touch our spirit.

Perhaps you've had this experience: You were involved in helping plan and celebrate an elaborate liturgy. You spent so much time in the preparations and were so preoccupied with making certain that things went well during the actual celebration, that the celebration itself was anti-climactic.

We can easily make the same mistake in teaching and celebrating liturgy with children. We can spend so much time in teaching about the meaning of the symbols, or in practicing the songs and rehearsing the actions, that the celebration itself is robbed of all mystery and spontaneity. The celebration becomes a performance rather than participation in the sacred actions and mystery of Jesus.

It is not suggested that liturgy should not be taught in our classes. Rather, what we need is to develop more trust in the power of good liturgy to speak for itself. Children by nature are much more experience-oriented than they are analytical. We should take a cue from them in striking a balance between experience and theory in teaching the liturgy.

A good rule of thumb teaching liturgy to children is this: It is better to provide the children with a good experience of a liturgical celebration than it is to have a carefully planned class about liturgy. Ideally, we strive to provide our children with both.

THEOLOGY UPDATE

Liturgy

People's relationship to worship in the Catholic Church has radically changed over the past twenty years. After years of background research, continued calls for the Mass to be celebrated in the vernacular, and a society that had rapidly moved into the modern era, the bishops gathered in council and on December 4, 1963, promulgated "The Constitution on the Liturgy."

Although sections of it now seem out of date, this first document not only gave us the outline for the reform of the liturgy but also gave the Church a model for looking at itself anew as Church, as people of God, as pilgrim.

Today we have the beginnings of a perspective to see where we have come from and what has happened to us as worshipers since that reform began. Insight into the liturgical changes comes from several vantage points: the revised rites themselves, the official introductions to them, the theological commentaries, and the actual varied modes of celebrations of these rites in the assemblies throughout our country and the world as a whole. Let's look at each of these factors.

The Revised Rites

After each rite was revised by Rome and written in Latin, it has been translated, approved, and implemented in each country of the world. Most noteworthy in the rites themselves is the importance of the word of God. No rite may be celebrated without first having a Liturgy of the Word. Gone are anointings, benediction, and penance celebrated in isolation from the Scriptures. The word is now related by homily to the particular situation. The word is also now celebrated with full use of the symbol that touches the assembly. (Full use suggests ample use of oil, Communion from the cup, and full laying on of hands, for instance.) The rites themselves are simpler, having fewer prayers and unnecessary duplications. They are to be celebrated by the entire assembly with ministers taking part in various parts — each doing only the part they are called to do. Finally, the rites are immediately understandable.

The Introductions (Praenotandi)

Admittedly the first rites that were revised had rather sketchy introductions. Each time another sacrament was revised, however, the introductions have become as important as the rites themselves, for they gave the tone, the intent, and the manner in which the rites are to be celebrated. While the rubrics still give the basic directions, the introductions explain the various options, the changes in attitude, and the circumstances for celebrating. For example, the "General Instruction" (paragraph 7) expands the understanding of the presence of Christ at Eucharist from the species alone, to his presence in the assembly, the word, and the presider.

Theological Commentaries

Academic and pastoral liturgies have done much to bring the liturgical movement to its present state. Their reflections and clarifications have helped celebrants adjust from "doing the sacrament for others" to "leading the assembly in the celebration of sacraments." They have provided guidelines for implementation, urged use of options, and formed liturgical ministers in the spirit of the celebrations they lead and participate in. The theological commentaries and the introduction have helped us to see the sacramental life of the Church as a "process" of conversion and growth culminating in the celebration of sacraments rather than the primary or sole means of grace followed by growth and conversion.

The Modes of Celebration

The people who have been exposed to good liturgical celebrations over a long period of time have changed. They are aware that they are part of the sacraments. They claim an ownership in the sacramental life of the Church. Good celebrations deepen their faith and convince them of the workings of God in their past and present life. Good liturgy, which relates the ever-present word of God to the ever-changing circumstances of people's pilgrimage, nourishes people so that they can live in truth and justice in the everyday marketplace of their lives.

From the 'Directory for Masses with Children'

"Even in the case of children, the liturgy itself always exerts its own proper didactic force. Yet, within programs of catechetical, scholastic, and parochial formation, the necessary importance should be given to catechesis on the Mass. This catechesis should be directed to the child's active, conscious, and authentic participation. 'Clearly accommodated to the age and mentality of the children, it should attempt, through the principal rites and prayers, to convey the meaning of the Mass, including a participation in the whole life of the Church.' This is especially true of the text of the eucharistic prayer and of the acclamations with which the children take part in this prayer" (No. 12).

"Various kinds of celebrations may also play a major role in the liturgical formation of children and in their preparation for the Church's liturgical life. By the very fact of celebration children easily come to appreciate some liturgical elements, for example, greetings, silence, and common praise (especially when this is sung in common). Such celebrations, however, should avoid having too didactic a character" (No. 13).

TEACHING TIPS

Use Your Bible Shrine

A good way to prepare the class each week for the following Sunday's liturgy is to divide the class into teams. Team One is responsible for the Bible shrine for the week.

1. They must read together the readings for the next Sunday's liturgy.

2. They must decide on its theme and decide on appropriate decorations for the shrine as suggested by the readings. For example,

a fish net, shocks of wheat, a poster depicting the story of the Gospel.

3. By Wednesday they should have the shrine decorated.

4. They must prepare a short explanation of the readings for that Sunday and decide how to present it.

5. On Friday they are allowed five minutes or so to give their presentation.

Next Monday it's Team Two's turn to go through the process. Repeat throughout the year.

Variation: To get the parents involved you could assign a single student with the same task. The student is expected to recruit parents to help him or her go through the steps: choose the theme, decide the decorations, prepare the report for the week. When possible invite the parent in on Friday to help give the report. Each week a different student/parent team is given the task.

Sacrament of the Week

A good way to teach or review all seven sacraments is this: Each week for seven weeks assign the sacrament of the week. With student help, decorate the bulletin board and the room with symbols, Scripture citations, and actual pictures related to the celebration of the sacrament of the week. On one day prepare and present to the class a brief history of the development of the sacrament through the ages. On another day review the ritual celebration of the sacrament. Read the prayers and share the explanations provided in the rite. Discuss the meaning of the symbols used. End the week with a mock celebration of the rite. A different group can be responsible for rehearsing and celebrating the rite.

When reconciliation is the sacrament of the week, it is a good idea for you to play the role of penitent for the mock celebration and for the parish priest to play the role of priest. It provides an excellent means for teaching students how to approach the sacrament. Attention is guaranteed!

When the Eucharist is the sacrament of the week, try to arrange for an actual celebration of it; a mock celebration is not appropriate here.

Thanksgiving

Have the students make Thanksgiving cards for their parents or guardians. They should write the word THANKSGIVING down one side of the page (for younger children, THANKS is sufficient). They should then try to come up with one word or phrase beginning with each of the letters that describes something for which they are grateful.

Let's use the following examples for the first three letters:

T = time spent with me
H = help with homework
A = always there when I need you

After they have their lists completed, have the students transpose these onto homemade Thanksgiving cards, decorated any way they wish. They should include their lists on the inside of the card.

As a continuation of this activity, now have the students write the word EUCHARIST down the side of a page. Explain that it, too, means *Thanks*. This time they should form a list of things God gives them for which they are grateful. These lists can then be used as the basis for making Thanksgiving posters to hang around the classroom. Students can decorate them as they see fit, but the theme should be gratitude for all God's gifts to them. Encourage the students to be personal rather than general.

Let the Students Do It

Share this simple formula for developing a prayer service with the students. Then teams of students can use it to develop prayer services for the class whenever appropriate. You will want to approve the final product, but don't take over the process from the group. Often the students will develop a prayer service that speaks very well to their age-group. Here's a working outline.

- Opening greeting and prayer.
- Scripture reading.
- Quiet reflection.
- Sung or spoken response to the reading.
- Second reading (optional).
- Quiet reflection.
- Sung or spoken response to the reading.
- Homily or shared reflection on the reading.
- Prayers of intercession.
- Shared gesture or use of one of the symbols.
- Concluding prayer.

More Than a Substitute

A good brief prayer for the closing of an activity is the ''Through Him, with Him, and in Him. . .'' at the end of the Canon. Use it in place of the Glory Be. Take time to explain it and its role in the Canon to the students. It is an excellent summary of the nature and purpose of the Mass.

Stump the Teacher

Provide the students with a LITURGICAL QUESTION BOX. Encourage the students to put in questions about the liturgy intended to stump the teacher. Encourage them to get questions from an encyclopedia or a catechism. Stress, however, that they must have the answers to the questions they submit and that they should sign their names to the questions. Each day draw out one question and attempt to answer it. Don't be embarrassed if you can't. That's half the fun and part of the learning experience. If you are stumped, the student who submitted the question must give the answer.

Students can learn a lot about the liturgy just looking up hard questions for you. The rest of the class can benefit when the answer is given.

Let's Hear It

The word of God plays a central role in all liturgy. A good way to help this age-group become more in touch with the word during the liturgy is to show how the word is used to develop key themes in celebration. You can start with one of the standard liturgies — for martyrs, confessors, etc. Or you may prefer a feast of Mary or one of the saints. Have the students read the assigned Scripture passages, including responses. Then discuss how the readings relate to the feast in question. What themes, ideas, virtues, or attitudes do they develop?

You can do the same thing by studying the readings for the Sundays in Advent and Lent.

As a variation assign the students a particular theme: Pro-Life, Peace and Disarmament, World Hunger. In groups have them peruse the Scriptures and select appropriate passages for the readings, including the responsorials. The groups can compare readings and decide upon the ones most suitable for the theme in question.

A good spin-off from this would be to have the students select appropriate hymns, develop prayers of the faithful, and suggest symbols and gestures that can be incorporated into the celebration to enhance the theme.

In this way the students begin to see how the whole celebration "holds together" while at the same time coming to appreciate the importance of the word of God in the celebration.

Why Not Memorize?

As a sneaky beginning for a more serious study of the Canon of the Mass, divide the class into groups. Each group is to memorize one of the three Canons in use today. Hold a recitation contest. Call on a volunteer from one of the groups. He or she begins. Then call on another to continue until the group gets through the whole Canon. Proceed with other groups. The group with the least mistakes wins.

Now you have a good basis for having the groups compare the similarities and differences between the three Canons. This leads into an explanation of essential elements of the Canon and their significance.

As a variation for making banners provide each student with a paper on which the outline of a Mass vestment and stole is drawn as shown at the left.

Assign each student a particular feast or season or a liturgical occasion — funeral, wedding, baptism. Have the students then decorate the vestments with appropriate liturgical symbols and words. Display the results around the room.

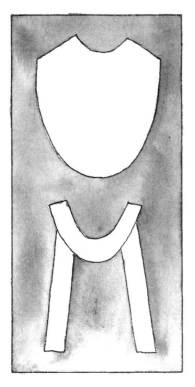

Peace to You

Begin by asking the students to discuss the various meanings or significance of the kiss of peace at Mass. These include, for example, forgiveness, acceptance, support, and affection. List the students' ideas on the board.

Now ask the students (in groups) if they can develop gestures or a new form of handshake that can express as many of the ideas behind the kiss of peace as possible.

Let the groups demonstrate, then allow the class to choose the best one. Incorporate it into the next liturgy you celebrate.

Sacrament Word Games

Have the students print the word *sacrament* vertically on a page. Ask each student to use the letters to form action words of love and friendship. For example:

```
      S hare
     l A ugh
       C all
   offe R
     c A re
  remeM ber
    list E n
    tha N k
       T hink about
   prai S e
```

Share and discuss each student's work. Display it afterward.

Variation: Do the same thing with the word *Eucharist*, asking the students to form action words of thanksgiving, celebration, and sharing; with the word *baptism*, forming words of welcome; with the word *reconciliation*, forming words of forgiveness and peace.

Symbols Speak

Take a tour of your parish church. Look for the various Christian symbols and where they are used. Encourage the students to sketch the symbols they find in their notebooks or on a special symbol-finding paper. Return to the classroom to discuss the meaning of some of the symbols (water, flame, tree or vine, bread/wine, grapes/wheat, dove). Where in the Bible do we find these symbols? Divide the class into groups and have each group design a church stained-glass window on butcher paper using the symbols collected. Instruct the groups to color the designs darkly with crayon, outlining and dividing the spaces with black felt-tip markers. Use a regular hair blow-dryer to melt the crayon into the paper. Mount the art window on a window or in a frame with a spotlight shining on it from the back. (The melted crayon on butcher paper becomes translucent.)

Making Jesus Present

Begin by reading the passage in Paul's First Letter to the Corinthians, 12:12-26. Discuss how each of us, united through baptism and the Eucharist, shares his or her life and is called to help make each of us present in the world through our actions. Now have the students recall and list the corporal and spiritual works of mercy.

Discuss practical things students their age can do that are in fact works of Jesus and ways to make Jesus present. On a large piece of butcher paper trace a silhouette (see accompanying illustration) and entitle it THE BODY OF JESUS.

Challenge the students during the next week to try to make Jesus present in their family, school, and/or neighborhood by doing some acts of kindness in his name. Remind the students as necessary during the next week. In about a week call on the students to share one deed they did in Jesus' name. They do this by writing it out on a slip of paper, unsigned. Collect the slips. Read them one by one and then pin each one on the silhouette.

Finally, invite each student to sign his or her name on the silhouette. End by reading 1 Corinthians 12:12-26 once again.

Signs of the Times

Invite the students to identify objects they would put in a time capsule that could symbolize today's youth culture to people finding the capsule two thousand years from now. Some examples might include a fast-food hamburger carton, a music tape of "We Are the World," and sneakers.

List their suggestions on the board. Then discuss each in turn to clarify what it symbolizes and whether or not the symbol chosen is the best symbol for that aspect of their culture. Refine the list as necessary. Now ask them to do the same activity, this time preparing a time capsule that would explain to people two thousand years from now what being Catholic means. Repeat the process of clarifying and refining the list. This provides a great opportunity to deal with deeper meanings of elements such as the Eucharist and other sacraments.

A New Holiday

Invite the students to develop a new national holiday. Give a few suggestions to get them started and then decide together on what holiday it will be. For example: National Hot Cocoa Day, National End of the School Year Day, or National Friendship Day. Once they have decided on the holiday, they will have to decide on the following: a slogan, a symbol, a gesture, and finally a simple community celebration.

Compare their finished product with one of the Church holidays to demonstrate how the Church uses the same kinds of symbolic methods to help people understand the meaning behind the feast day.

In Olden Times

Here's an approach to teaching sacramentals and Church traditions. Ask the students to seek from their parents, grandparents, or other older relatives, religious articles they may have in the house. Compose a list like the following to help them know what to ask for:

- Medals, scapulars.
- Statues, religious pictures, holy cards.
- Rosaries.
- Holy-water bottle.
- Novena prayer books or cards.
- Devotional prayer books.
- Older missals with the Latin and English in them.

Instruct the students to prepare a short written report explaining their object: how it was used, how the person felt about using it, the origin of the object or devotion (if appropriate).

Call on volunteers to share their reports either by reading the written report or by speaking about it extempore. Create a display corner in which the items are placed for viewing.

Be careful to ensure that the objects are returned. Also, be sure that even the "out-of-date" objects and practices are treated with respect, as having played an important part in aiding people in their faith life at a certain time in history.

Variation: Ask the students to do reports on certain customs and practices that were common to faith life prior to the Second Vatican Council. They should do their research by interviewing older Catholics. Possible topics include:

- The Communion fast "starting at midnight."
- The Lenten fast.
- Forty hours.
- Ember days.
- Rogation days.
- Corpus Christi procession.
- Any other customs and practices you feel appropriate.

After the students share their research, discuss the role of holy days and religious customs today.

Appreciation Day

Begin now to plan an Appreciation Day to be held toward the end of the school year. Your class can take the initiative, but you will want to eventually involve other classes as well.

Begin by asking the students to try to list as many people as they can in the school or parish who help in the work of Jesus but usually in ways that go unnoticed. The list might include the janitor, school and/or parish secretary, cafeteria workers, people who clean and decorate the church, crossing guards, and bus drivers. You can be as expansive or limited as you desire. With student help, design APPRECIATION CERTIFICATES, possibly tailored to each individual by including a symbol of that person's contribution. Some examples could include a janitor's broom and a secretary's typewriter.

If feasible, plan a short assembly in which each person will be honored by the whole school as the certificates are given. If this is not practical, arrange to have small groups of students hand deliver the certificates.

Chapter 6
Scripture

The relationship between religious education and Scripture is similar to the relationship between glove and hand. A glove not filled with a hand is lifeless. Religious education classes not permeated with the message of Scripture are also without life. This doesn't mean that we must enter every class, Bible in hand, quoting chapter and verse at each step in our lesson.

But there are a few questions we can ask ourselves to check on how effectively we are integrating Scripture into our classes.

1. Do I have a Bible enshrined in an appropriate place in the classroom?

Whenever possible this visible sign of reverence for the Scripture should be made present to our students. It has a wholesome effect on all age-groups, nurturing their own reverence for God's word.

2. Do I personally reverence the Scripture as a kind of sacrament, a means for coming into contact with God and experiencing his word in my life?

If this is our conviction, then any time we do introduce a passage of Scripture into our lessons or prayers it will come through to our children. We thus enable them to personally experience the power of God's word in their own lives. We must trust that the word will always have a more powerful effect on them than anything we can say. We thus allow God to speak for himself directly to our children.

3. Do I recognize that the central message contained in all of Scripture is one of God's unconditional love for us and his continual efforts to secure our well-being (our friendship with him)?

Using individual stories or passages taken from Scripture can be an effective means for teaching a particular truth or moral lesson. Jesus himself did this often. However, our ultimate goal is to help our children recognize the central message of all Scripture — God loves us and actively seeks our happiness. It would be unfortunate if we *only* used Scripture as a tool for stressing some isolated truth or moral value. We must always be concerned about helping our children discover and experience the central message when we use Scripture in our lessons.

4. Am I at least moderately informed about what contemporary Scripture scholarship teaches us regarding the interpretation and understanding of Scripture?

God's word to us must be filtered through things like literary styles, symbolic language, an author's purpose for writing, cultural influences on the choice of words and images, the overall process of Scripture's development into its final form. We don't have to be Scripture scholars, but we need to at least be aware of the basic skills of exegesis (interpretation of Scripture). We must also share these skills with our children at appropriate times. Even Jesus was often misunderstood and misquoted when his contemporaries interpreted his words in a too literal sense.

5. Do I appreciate the essential role the word of God has in all sacramental celebrations, in the liturgical seasons and symbols? Scripture is the foundation of our liturgical theology and is central to our liturgical life. It is within the context of liturgical celebration that God's word is most powerfully proclaimed and experienced. It is important, therefore, to give special emphasis to the role of Scripture as we engage in sacrament preparation, teach lessons on the sacraments and the liturgical seasons, or prepare our children for any Eucharistic celebration.

Chances are, you can give at least a qualified "yes" to all the above questions. Assuming that's true, rest assured that you are effectively incorporating Scripture into your religion classes.

THEOLOGY UPDATE

Sacred Scripture

History of Interpretation

What is the hidden meaning of the text? How can we decode the words of Scripture to make them timely for our situation? These were questions that many Fathers of the Church posed as they sought to unravel the word of God for their communities. Their method was allegorical, that is, the Scriptures were a cryptogram, an extended metaphor. For example, in the Parable of the Good Samaritan (Luke 10:25-37) Augustine identified the man as Adam, Jerusalem as the heavenly city of peace, and Jericho as the symbol of mortality. In the Parable of the Sower (Matthew 13:4-23; Mark 4:1-20; Luke 8:4-15) both Augustine and Jerome interpreted widows as the sixty percent and the married as the forty percent. For Jerome the one hundred percent meant chaste women, while for Augustine they were the martyrs.

In the Middle Ages Thomas Aquinas recognized the importance of the literal meaning, that is, what the sacred author actually intended to communicate. However, despite some exceptions, the allegorical school ruled the day at the close of that period. To make matters worse, there was an ever deepening chasm between theology and the interpretation of the biblical text. Unfortunately, efforts at translating the Bible into the vernacular often had heretical overtones.

With the advent of the Protestant Reformation in the sixteenth century, both Catholics and Protestants stressed the historical background of the biblical works and the centrality of the literal sense. To cite one example, the Jesuit Johannes Maldonatus published some outstanding scriptural commentaries. Once the danger from the Reformation subsided, Catholics resorted to the spiritual interpretation of the allegorical school. In Protestantism, too, the Bible was often reduced to a manual of asceticism.

In the nineteenth and twentieth centuries the literal interpretation regained its proper place. The archaeological discoveries from the world of the ancient Near East drew attention to the fact that the Old Testament did not arise in splendid isolation. As an anthology of literature, it shared a common heritage while differing from the environment because of its faith stance. Similarly the Gospels emerged in a new light. They were not blow-by-blow historical accounts of Jesus of Nazareth. Rather, they were efforts to interpret the impact and significance of Jesus for later and indeed different audiences.

Recent Church Pronouncements

In 1943 Pope Pius XII issued the encyclical "Divino Afflante Spiritu," often hailed as the Magna Charta of Catholic biblical interpretation. In this document the pope urged the need to appreciate the literary forms used by the biblical writers. Thus parables, psalms of lament, letters, and popular stories implied approaching reality from different vantage points. The Book of Jonah is not the story of a whale but a powerful parable about God's will to save and his refusal to be shackled by human limitations. The Song of Songs does not recite the allegory of the love affair between Yahweh and Israel but the adventures and depth of the erotic love affair between a man and a woman.

In 1964 the Pontifical Biblical Commission published the "Instruction on the Historical Truth of the Gospels." This document stressed the three stages by which Jesus' life and teaching have come down to us. These stages are: (1) Jesus; (2) the early Church proclaiming and developing the centrality of Jesus; and (3) the evangelists shaping and interpreting the two earlier stages to meet the needs of their communities.

In the Parable of the Sower the focus in stage No. 1 is on the seed. Jesus, probably reacting to the limited reception of his message, points to the law of growth and decline in the kingdom. God's mysterious plan is at work: good results do come, although the bad ones are more easily explained. In stage No. 2 the early Church interpreted these gains and losses as reflecting the different dispositions of people (receiving the word with joy but without roots, being choked by life's anxieties, etc.). In stage No. 3 Luke adds to the condition of the good seed the note of perseverance.

In 1965, in its "Dogmatic Constitution on Divine Revelation," the Second Vatican Council reaffirmed these stages in the transmission of the Gospels.

The Modern Roman Catholic

The Bible has regained its central place in the life of the Church as a whole and in the lives of individuals. The reform of the lectionary now introduces worshipers to a large segment of the Old Testament and to all four Gospels (Matthew no longer has the lion's share). Churchgoers now expect the homilist to comment on the biblical readings and develop their relevance for daily living. Biblical preaching is clearly in vogue.

Courses on the Bible are no longer limited to the seminary or schools of theology. They attract audiences on the college level where they have alerted many to the richness of biblical experience and thought. On both the elementary and high school levels the Bible is also finding its proper place. Parish discussion and study groups likewise see in the Bible various opportunities for enrichment and growth.

The desired fruit of this biblical renewal is to see the Bible more as an inciter of questions than a provider of answers. The biblical experience is calculated to have the believer assess his or her faith commitment against the background of the past and to dare to ask new questions. It is no longer acceptable to determine only what Jesus said or did or what the evangelist chose to present Jesus as saying or doing. One must seek to determine how the biblical experience can challenge modern living. Ultimately the message must shock us, upset us, and move us in the direction of asking new questions for our new world. Only in this way will we be not only the heirs of the biblical past but also the promoters of the biblical future.

John F. Craghan
College of Great Falls
Great Falls, Montana

TEACHING TIPS

Seek and Find

This can challenge your imagination as much as it challenges your students. Using old religion books, calendars, magazines, and newspapers, find pictures that can be related to some incident or story in Scripture. Some examples would be:

- A whale (Jonah, Jesus' foretelling of his resurrection).
- A fancy robe, multicolored (Joseph).
- Frogs, flies, or locusts (one of the plagues).
- Dry lake bed (crossing of the Red Sea).

We told you it would be a challenge. Give the students, in small groups, one of the pictures and instruct them to try to find a Scripture passage that is suggested by the picture. They should cite chapter and verse and be prepared to explain their choice.

Variation: Give the students, again in small groups, the citation for a Scripture episode. Provide them with magazines and other sources of pictures. They must find a picture that could be used with that episode and be prepared to explain their choice.

The Way of the Cross

Give the students a list of the fifteen stations (''fifteenth'' is the Resurrection). Using the four Gospels, the students must find an appropriate Scripture passage that could be used for each station. If you wish, you could allow them to use the Old Testament, directing them especially to the Psalms, Lamentations, and Isaiah.

After the students have selected their Scripture passage they should also compose a short prayer that could be used with each station. Often this works best if you assign small groups responsibility for one station only.

A Special Word

After impressing on the students that the Gospels (all Scripture) are really God's word to us today, instruct each student to search for and choose *one* saying or verse that the student feels is what God wants to say to him or her at this time.

Allow the students to then reproduce the verse in some artistic way on poster paper — from words and letters cut from newspapers and magazines, potato printing (each student cuts one letter from a potato and all share the letters — good community builder if you can tolerate the confusion); crayon scraping (color the entire poster paper with crayon and scrape out letters); etc. Ask the students to explain the reasons for their choice to the class. Encourage the students to post their finished product in some prominent place at home (refrigerator door, for example) so that they can share it with the family. They might want to incorporate the verse into meal prayers.

Still True Today

Provide the students with a copy of the beatitudes. Instruct them, with the help of their parents, to search through the local newspaper or weekly newsmagazine to find at least one example of each beatitude being lived out today as reported in a news story.

Variation: Working with the Ten Commandments, find examples of the commandment being obeyed or violated. Even with this age-group you can have some interesting sharing and also makes for good parental involvement and education.

TV Producer

Divide the class into groups to work on this project. Each group is assigned a Scripture episode being currently studied. They must translate the Scripture story into a TV show. Materials for each group: cardboard box with bottom cut out; two broomsticks or wood dowels; roll of butcher paper or roll of similar paper (to be shared as needed among groups); marking pens or crayons. *Optional:* pictures from magazines, scissors, and paste. The task is to develop a script and visuals to tell the story assigned. Some groups may be creative enough to use a tape recorder for music background.

Include time for commercials, some of which can be quite funny. Parents, usually fathers, should be involved in helping to construct the TV set.

Let There Be Maps

Intermediate and junior-high students tend to love maps. Use them when dealing with Scripture. The students will become absorbed in geography, finding out about flora and fauna, climate, the details of the region in which the Scripture story unfolded.

Scripture Captions

The following activity can help your students become more involved in discovering meaning in Scripture. Gather a collection of pictures from old magazines and calendars. Form the class into teams and give each team several of your pictures. Ask the teams to search through Scripture and select an appropriate Scripture passage as a caption to go with each picture. They can paste the picture on a piece of poster board and print their quote below it, then show and explain their choices.

This can also be done with students working individually. You can also limit the section of Scripture to be used if you happen to be focusing on a particular book or topic; for example, a prophet, the Psalms, the Sermon on the Mount, the Covenant. As a variation you can provide the Scripture quotes (as well as old magazines and calendars) and instruct the students to find pictures that can go with the quotes.

Chapter 7
Jesus

No matter what specific topics we are asked to present (for example, sacraments, Scripture, Church, and prayer), Jesus remains central to our catechesis. Let's review a few principles that can help us in our efforts to keep our catechesis Christ-centered.

A basic principle is to remain sensitive to the children's present capacity to understand and relate to Jesus. On the practical level, this means we must continually ask ourselves two questions as we prepare to talk about Jesus in our classes:

1. What truths, facts, and personal qualities or attributes of Jesus are important to stress in relation to this topic?

2. How can we best translate this information into examples, stories, and images appropriate for the age-group we are teaching?

For younger children, we need to continually reinforce the idea that Jesus is real and historical, and to relate him to the child's real world of joys and hurts rather than to the child's fantasy world.

For older children, too, but for different reasons, we need to focus primarily on Jesus as a historical person, as God-become-flesh. Strive to present a Jesus who is approachable, who shares in and understands our human condition, and who remains actively involved in our day-to-day concerns.

This leads to the second principle. The best source for our information about Jesus remains the Gospel accounts. Mark's Gospel is especially good at portraying Jesus in this tangible human way without sacrificing the truth of his divinity. Therefore, draw heavily upon the Gospels. Read from them directly or paraphrase, but, as much as possible, use actual Gospel events and descriptions when presenting Jesus. In short, try to present Jesus within the setting of first-century Palestine. Enrich your stories about Jesus with factual details about the circumstances and customs of the society in which he lived among us. This is helpful for both younger and older children. Any "research" you do that gives you such background information will greatly enhance your ability to present Jesus to any age-group.

In terms of relating the various miracles of Jesus, several points should be kept in mind. Be careful to put the emphasis on the motive or purpose of the miracle and the good it accomplished. Jesus never did miracles to call attention to himself or impress others with supernatural powers. He used this power, entrusted to him by the Father, primarily to aid and heal those in need. Also take the time, when possible, to situate a particular miracle within its Gospel context, especially with older children. The evangelists carefully chose each miracle they presented and had a particular purpose for presenting it when they did. Random, unsituated stories about the miraculous powers of Jesus can give children a distorted view and can be a disservice rather than an aid to the child's understanding of Jesus.

Another principle to remember is this: Do not hesitate to "model" for the children how to relate to Jesus. Share your own relationship to Jesus with your students. Talk freely about what he means to you, the role he plays in your life, how to pray to and in other ways relate to him. Describe those tangible qualities or attributes about Jesus that you personally find most attractive and comforting. Your own real relationship with Jesus, shared candidly, will be perhaps one of the best ways to demonstrate to your children that a personal relationship with Jesus is both possible and desirable.

In this regard there is one final principle: Always strive to present a balanced view of Jesus just as the Gospels do. Though clearly devoted to the poor and outcast, Jesus reached out to the rich and well-placed, too. He was gentle and forgiving; he could be stern, and he could display a rightful anger. He was a man of prayer; he was a man of action. Women and men were equally comfortable in his presence. So were children and the elderly, the strong and the weak. He could communicate with the uneducated and dialogue with scholars. He was equally at ease at a banquet table and around a campfire. While each of us will naturally tend to be drawn by certain dimensions of Jesus' person, we must be careful not to stress our particular bias at the expense of Jesus' other qualities. Jesus can attract everyone — provided we present him holistically.

In summary, when you present Jesus to your students keep these principles in mind:

- Adapt your presentation to the children's age level.
- Seek to focus on the tangible and historical.
- Root your presentations in Scripture.
- "Model" your own personal relationship with Jesus.
- Strive to maintain a balanced view of Jesus.

To the degree that we regularly introduce the children to the person of Jesus throughout our lessons, we will be effective catechists no matter what else we teach.

The Historical Jesus

Probably one of the most exciting aspects of Scripture scholarship and related disciplines today is the attempt to rediscover the historical Jesus — an authentic portrait of Jesus, the carpenter's son from Nazareth who lived in first-century Palestine.

In the past several decades, an incredible amount of research has taken place regarding the New Testament texts and just about every aspect of history and archaeology related to first-century Palestine. Armed with this new information and the insights of modern New Testament exegesis, scholars have been attempting to gain new insight into the person of Jesus, precisely as a first-century Galilean Jew.

In these attempts, one theological question is central: Being fully human as well as fully divine, did Jesus in fact have to learn like each of us? Did he have to discover his vocation as the Messiah, and if so, when did he discover it? Did his mission evolve in his own mind in response to circumstances and new insights, or did he have a clear plan for his mission from childhood onward? To what extent was Jesus' formation and consequently his mission influenced by the culture, religious movements, and politics of his times? For example, was he influenced by the Essene community as John the Baptizer apparently was? Was he sympathetic to the Zealot movement?

None of these questions have much significance if we opt for one theologically acceptable premise, namely that Jesus had direct access to divine knowledge from infancy onward by virtue of his own divinity.

A large number of scholars today, however, lean toward the premise that Jesus in his humanity learned like each of us. By drawing on both New Testament exegesis and theological principles, many hold that Jesus did acquire knowledge about himself and his mission in human fashion. In the process, he was significantly shaped by his cultural surroundings like any person would be.

On the other hand, we should be aware that no one has come up with an acceptable theological formula for explaining the relationship between Jesus' human and divine knowledge.

In any case, while many scholars agree that Jesus learned in a human fashion, agreement tends to end there. Using the evidence at hand, some argue, for example, that Jesus was actually a political revolutionary and possibly even a member of the Zealot party. While not necessarily a promoter of violent revolution, he actively sought political and economic reform. Others challenge this concept. They identify him more closely with the ideals of the Essene community, which upheld a strict observance of the covenant laws. They see Jesus as having little interest in political or social reform as such, except inasmuch as this would come about by a return to an authentic observance of the Jewish covenant.

Some scholars suggest that Jesus at first felt his mission would be successful and that he would be able to convert the Jewish people en masse to acceptance of the reign of God and the new era he had been sent to usher in. Only gradually did he begin to realize that this was not to be. He had to come to grips with the fact that he would be killed. His faith and hope in Yahweh were tested to the full in the process. Some suggest that Jesus had to struggle with doubts about himself, for example, that his conviction that he was the Messiah might be self-delusion!

Other scholars emphasize the fact that Jesus was a Galilean and use this to explain certain aspects of his mission and his teaching. For example, Galileans in general were known to have a rather cosmopolitan approach to life and associated more freely with the Gentiles than other Jews. The religious reforms of the Pharisees were influential primarily in Judea. Galileans weren't noted for strict observance. As a Galilean, Jesus would have been suspect from the start in Jerusalem. As a Galilean, he would have instinctively found the excessive formalism of the Pharisees bothersome and inauthentic.

What are we to make of this kind of scholarship today? Two guidelines can be helpful. First, don't be scandalized by the speculations of theologians. Some of their insights and promises may be jarring when they challenge some of our own long-standing presuppositions about Jesus. But if their insights serve to stimulate us to continually seek to know Jesus better, they are doing us a real service. Second, seek to maintain a balanced perspective. Any premise about Jesus that narrows rather than expands our understanding of Jesus deserves to be challenged. In this area, take your cues from the evangelists. What they did not tell us about Jesus is as significant as what they did tell us. Perhaps Jesus was sympathetic to the Zealot cause and his mission was affected by their ideals. However, none of the evangelists saw fit to say that. We can only surmise that either that fact was not critical for their readers' understanding of this preaching, or it was actually detrimental to understanding it.

Ultimately, as helpful and exciting as some of this current scholarship is in deepening our understanding of Jesus, we will never be able to "define" Jesus or reduce his messages to some "ism" that can be explained by his psychological makeup and cultural surroundings.

While it is true that Jesus is fully human and was enfleshed in a particular time and place in our human history, he remains the Word of God who is thus enfleshed.

Contemporary scholarship is proving to be an invaluable aid in helping us penetrate deeper into the mystery of the person and message of Jesus. But it does not seek nor can it ever claim to be able to reduce Jesus or his message to purely human dimensions. If we approach the works of today's scholars with that in mind, they can help us greatly in our faith quest: To know Christ Jesus.

TEACHING TIPS

What Are You Saying?

With the help of your students, look through the Gospels and identify fifteen or twenty of the short sayings of Jesus. Invite the students to paraphrase them. Ask one student to copy the "approved" paraphrase onto 3" x 5" cards, one saying to a card. For example:

- You can judge a tree by its fruit.
- You are worth more than many sparrows.
- Don't hide your light under a bushel.
- The good shepherd is willing to die for the sheep.
- Bad actions come from bad thoughts.

Use the task of paraphrasing the Gospel sayings as an opportunity for the students to discuss the meanings of these sayings. Let individuals or teams suggest various paraphrases for the original saying and have the whole class choose the one that comes closest to the original meaning.

Variation: Give the students citations from the New Testament as the starting point of the activity. They must first look up the citation before they try to paraphrase it.

Collect the cards and try this in a later class. Divide the class into teams. Play charades using the cards as the topics for the students to act out. Keep time and score as in Charades, the TV game show of past fame. After a team identifies the saying correctly, a volunteer from that team must be able to explain the meaning of the saying before the team gets its points.

Variation: Have a student draw a card and read the saying, then have small groups discuss and come up with one *practical application* for that saying in their present situation: home, school, neighborhood, with friends, etc. Ask the groups to share their responses. Encourage the students to actually try to put the saying into practice in one of the ways suggested.

Golden Oldie

If you haven't done this perennial favorite with your class, it is always an exciting activity. Discuss together the meaning of Easter and the Good News we are all asked to proclaim as a result of Jesus' resurrection. Have the students then translate their ideas into a short message of Good News and write this on a small piece of paper. Put the message (together with your name and the grade you teach, plus the name and address of the school) into a small plastic pill container like the kind druggists use, then obtain a helium-filled balloon and attach the pill container securely to it. In the context of a short, outdoor prayer service on the themes of Easter and apostleship, release your balloon. Wait for a week or so to see if anyone finds the message and contacts you.

Variation: You may wish to divide the class into smaller groups and have each group release its own message and balloon. Or you may wish to invite other classes to join you and have each class release its own message and balloon.

Two for One

A good way to conduct an end-of-the-year review and also present a practical project for summer is this. Have the students review each chapter in their textbook. This can be done in small groups if you wish. For each chapter, the groups are to identify one important truth or idea and one important Christian practice that the chapter teaches. You can have them identify more than one of each if you prefer. List these on the board in two columns as they are reported.

Discuss each truth listed to determine what it actually means and why they chose it as an important one. This helps review and clarify the main ideas of the chapter. Next, discuss the practices listed. Have the students discuss how each of these could be done during the coming summer months in a *practical* way. Now provide each student with a small envelope and 3" x 5" card. On the envelope they are to write their summer address. On the card they are to write two practices from the list on the board that they plan to carry out in some way during the summer months. Ask them to sign the cards and place them in the envelope, unsealed.

At some time during the summer send these cards to them together with a little greeting and a reminder to try to carry out what they promised. It is a nice personal touch, and it helps keep the fruits of your religion class alive throughout the summer.

Names of Jesus

Have the students try to recall as many "names" or titles of Jesus as they can from both the Old and New Testaments. For example: Good Shepherd, Lamb of God, Messiah, Rabbi, Master, Priest, Prophet, King, Son of Man, Son of God, Light of the World, Way, Truth, and Life.

List these on the board as they are given. Invite the students to choose one of these titles and compose a word picture using the following format:

Title
Adjective, Adjective
Verb and Object
Adjective, Adjective
Noun

For example:

Messiah
Promised, Awaited
Destroys Sin
Strong, Gentle
Savior

Variation: A less poetic but equally challenging activity would be to have older students make crossword puzzles in which the names and titles of Jesus are the answers. This requires that they think of good clues or definitions in order to describe the name or title.

Madison Avenue — A.D. 33

A fun way to get this age-group to do research on the culture and customs that existed in Jesus' day is to have the students (alone or in groups) develop newspaper or radio advertisements for goods and services that existed during Jesus' time in Palestine, including housing, transportation, clothes, tools, farm equipment, fishing equipment, help-wanted ads, and sporting or recreational events.

Everything You Wanted to Know

Instruct the students to write down the three questions they would most like to ask Jesus if they could meet him face-to-face. Questions can be unsigned if you prefer. Discourage inconsequential questions such as: "Who's going to win the Super Bowl?" Collect the lists and compile them into groupings of similar questions. Deal with one of these questions each time an occasion warrants it — as a "filler" activity toward the end of a session or as a regular "Ask God" activity at a set time each week.

What's Going On?

Divide the class into groups of five or six. Assign each group an episode or parable from the Gospels, but stress that each group should keep secret the passage they are working on.

Have the groups read over the episode and work up a way to pantomime it for the class.

They cannot speak at all during the presentation and cannot use props other than what they may have available in the classroom. For example, a row of desks can be arranged to be a boat, etc., but keep props to a minimum.

Allow sufficient time for the groups to develop their presentation; however, make it clear that the presentation itself should not last longer than a maximum of three minutes.

As each group completes its pantomime the rest of the class should then try to guess which Gospel episode or parable was being acted out.

After the groups have given their presentations, you may invite the class to pick the "best" presentation.

Variation: Assign the groups various episodes of the Gospel and provide them with small paper bags. Have the groups read over their episode, identify the various characters in it, and then decorate the bags with Magic Markers to depict each of the characters. Additional materials such as yarn for hair and beards can be provided if you wish. Have the groups then use their bag people as hand puppets to reenact their episode for the class in their own words.

Even the older, more inhibited students can enter into the spirit of the "play" when using such hand puppets. It also gives a good insight into how well the students understand the meaning behind the episode.

Some good episodes include the Woman at the Well, the Story of Zacchaeus, the Prodigal Son, the Man Born Blind, the Wedding Feast at Cana, and the Raising of Lazarus.

What Kind of Friend Am I?

Ask the students to look up the following New Testament quotes:
- John 2:1-12 (The Wedding at Cana).
- Mark 10:13-16 (Blessing of the Children).
- Mark 6:30-33 (The Return of the Twelve).
- John 18:1-14 (Jesus Arrested).
- John 21:1-14 (The Appearance to the Seven Disciples).

Have the students discuss the *practical* quality of Jesus' friendship as illustrated in each of these episodes. Then have them complete the following sentence with a word or phrase that "captures" the aspect of Jesus' friendship the episode illustrates: "As a friend Jesus is always. . ."

Variation: Have the students illustrate the episode in the form of a poster. For a caption, have them develop a sentence that captures a certain aspect of Jesus' friendship.

Challenge the students to find other episodes in the Gospels that illustrate the kind of practical friend Jesus is to us.

Evaluation: A simple way to get a feel for what the students gained from your class this year is the "complete the sentence" approach. Develop a number of sentence starters based on the key themes (and other material) you covered during the year. Ask the students to complete these as seriously and honestly as they can. To get more candid responses from older students, allow them to submit the work unsigned. Here are some sample sentence starters:

- The most important thing I learned about the sacrament of reconciliation was. . .
- What I learned most about how to pray was. . .
- The thing that most impressed me in learning about Jesus was. . .
- The most important thing I learned about the Church was. . .
- The thing I liked most about this class was. . .
- The thing I liked most about our teacher was. . .

Develop your own sentences based on what you wish to find out. Present as many sentences as you wish.

Chapter 8
The Holy Spirit

To teach about the Holy Spirit is perhaps the most challenging task of a catechist. Children can picture God as Father and can personally relate characteristics attributed to him through their own experience of parents and other adults. God the Son, having become flesh, is sufficiently "tangible" for even little children to grasp. (We can even draw pictures of Jesus.) But God the Spirit? Traditional images like fire and wind — or even a more tangible image like a dove — don't help much. While there is no guaranteed approach that is effective, here's one approach that may be useful in your attempts to help the children form an understanding of — and a relationship with — the Holy Spirit.

Everyone has a kind of inner spirit of personality. We communicate our personality or spirit to others through our words, gestures, and actions. In the process of projecting our personality, we influence others. Others influence us by their personalities in much the same way. You've undoubtedly noticed how a particular person can enter a room and almost immediately the mood of the group becomes upbeat. Persons who have an essentially optimistic, enthuasistic, and outgoing personality will inevitably influence a group in this upbeat way. A sullen, selfish, cynical, or hypercritical person, on the other hand, will usually create negative influence through the force of his or her personality. Calm and thoughtful persons will bring an air of composure and steadiness to a group.

This ability each of us has to influence others is in a real sense the process of sharing or sending our own "spirit" to others. To the degree that they are open and allow it, our spirit will touch them and influence their own spirit and their own behavior. At the same time, they discover who we really are because we have revealed our innermost personality or spirit to them.

There is a valid analogy between this everyday reality of human interaction and the role of the Spirit of God in our lives. The Spirit is like God's "personality." To come under the influence of God's Spirit is to be influenced by the "personality" of God. By recognizing the effect God's Spirit has on us, we come to know more about God's inner self and true nature.

Let us examine the analogy further. When God "enters the room," we begin to experience the effects of his personality, otherwise called the fruits of his Spirit: love, joy, peace, patience, kindness, goodness, faith, modesty, and continence. To the degree that we are open and allow God's personality to influence us, we share in the very power of that personality, otherwise called the gifts of the Spirit: wisdom, understanding, knowledge, counsel, fortitude (courage), reverence, and fear of the Lord (that is, a correct ordering of our priorities and a true appreciation for our relationship to God). When we reflect on the fruits and gifts — that is, the kind of influence God's personality exerts on us — we come to know God more directly. God is peace and patience. God is love and joy. God is wisdom and understanding. God is gentleness and fidelity. By the middle grades and upward, this analogy can begin to be an effective means for explaining the nature and role of the Spirit of God. Also, traditional images of the Spirit can be related to this analogy. We talk about people having a fiery, passionate, or warm personality. Fire is an apt image for the kind of "personality" God possesses. We talk about people who have a free, unpredictable, forceful, vital, energizing personality. The unfettered breeze, the roaring wind, the rhythmic breath of life — these are all apt images of God's personality.

To test out the appropriateness of this analogy, try this little exercise yourself or involve your students in it. Find suitable passages in Scripture that deal with references to the Spirit or to the Spirit's activity — for example, "And they were all filled with the holy Spirit. . . . Then Peter stood up . . . and proclaimed. . ." (Acts 2:4). Many, but certainly not all passages, will lend themselves to a kind of paraphrase such as "And Peter, under the influence of God's personality, spoke up. . . ." or "And Peter, under God's personal influence, spoke up. . . ."

Now an important word of caution. The Spirit is a divine Person, coequal and coeternal with the Father and the Son. In using this analogy we don't deny this essential truth of our faith. We are simply trying to find another way to help children (and adults) understand the Spirit's relationship to the Father and the Son and the Spirit's role in the redemptive action of God. Try to remember at all times that we are dealing with an analogy. The Spirit of God *is like* or functions *like* or influences *like* the personality of a human person. The Spirit of God *is not* simply a collection of "divine personality traits." To the degree that this analogy makes sense to you and you are comfortable with it, you will find it helpful to have it in your catechetical repertoire. If this approach doesn't seem all that clear to you, there are other ways to approach this mystery. No one approach will ever adequately embrace all that can be said about the Spirit.

Finally, in your attempts to teach your students about the Spirit, always turn to the same Spirit for help and guidance. Who better than the Holy Spirit can instruct you in how to present God to others?

THEOLOGY UPDATE

Pentecost

Pentecost is the culminating feast of the Paschal season. There are two aspects of this feast that have special significance for our catechesis. First, Pentecost marks the "debut of the Holy Spirit" in the life of the Church. Second, it marks the "birthday" of the Church itself. Let's examine each of these briefly.

Clearly, the Spirit's presence and activity are referred to throughout Scripture, starting in the very first verses of Genesis. But the concept of the Spirit as a distinct Person of the Godhead was foreign to the Old Testament mentality. In the Gospels — written after the Pentecost event — references to the Spirit take on a more personal character. But it is especially at Pentecost that the Spirit, foretold and promised by Jesus, actually becomes manifest as a distinct Person. There he clearly assumes the role as guide and guardian of the Church, whose very existence he effects and confirms, both at the same time. At Pentecost, the Spirit is present with transforming power. He is experienced as the very fruit of the Redemption longed for in the Old Testament and recently achieved through the death and resurrection of Jesus. The Spirit is experienced as the gift of new life that Jesus won for us in abundance. The Spirit's presence is marked by a transformation of those who receive it. The disciples at Pentecost are described as energized, empowered, even compelled to proclaim the salvation they experience.

Once "released," the Spirit can't be controlled or suppressed. As the Spirit of Jesus, he assumes leadership of Jesus' Church. He goes before it into the world and draws the Apostles after him. When you read Acts, it seems the Apostles are hard pressed to keep up. Time after time, they arrive at a place only to find the Spirit had preceded them. Just as often, they are clearly instructed by the Spirit where to go next. The Acts of the Apostles is often described as the "Gospel of the Holy Spirit." Beginning at Pentecost, then, the Spirit's role in the redemptive process becomes clearly established. He is the fruit of salvation — the gift of new life won for us by Jesus. He is the guide of the community of the saved, whose mission is to bear witness to the good news of salvation. The Spirit does not leave this important mission to chance. He clearly takes charge and directs it. He is also the guardian of the new community, intervening as necessary to protect it from error and from the forces of evil that would impede or destroy it. From his "debut" at Pentecost onward, the Spirit remains with the Church — as the fruit of salvation, as the guide, and as the guardian.

It is not surprising that this "debut" of the Spirit also marks the "birthday" of the Church. To understand this, however, we must look first to the Old Testament. The Passover-Exodus experience marked God's intervention to save the Hebrews from Egyptian slavery and oppression. This redemptive act did not end on the other side of the Red Sea. A mysterious, luminous cloud guided and protected the escapees, finally leading them to Mount Sinai. There, amidst wind and fire, God established a covenant with those he had saved. He sealed them as his own, forming them into a people. The covenant experience completed (that is, confirmed) God's redemptive process. It was the "birthday" of the Israelites, God's Chosen People.

This Paschal event of the Old Testament is the prototype of the ultimate salvation achieved in Jesus. Jesus' death-resurrection marks our own exodus from the slavery and death effected by sin. But it is at Pentecost that this redemptive process is completed. At Pentecost, the faithful disciples are covenanted and sealed as the New People of God. Their faith and their salvation are confirmed. The Church is born. It is no accident that the evangelist uses the same images of wind and fire that accompanied the Sinai experience to describe this new covenanting experience.

At Sinai, the "first" Pentecost (also known as the Jewish holiday of Shabuoth), the Israelites received the covenant's law to guide and guard them. At the new Pentecost, the Church receives the Spirit himself to be her law, guide, and guardian. The Israelites, as God's Chosen People, were expected to conform their lives to the law. The New People of God are expected to conform to the Spirit who remains present in their midst. The law of the Old Testament was written on stones. The New Testament law is written in our hearts where the Spirit now dwells.

In the same way, just as Pentecost must be viewed as the culmination of the Paschal event begun at Jesus' death-resurrection, so our personal sacramental participation in the Paschal event, begun at our baptism, is completed at our confirmation. The birth of the New People of God was begun in blood on Calvary and confirmed in the fire at the Cenacle. Our own birth as members of the Church is begun in the waters of baptism and confirmed by the energizing, sealing oils of confirmation. The Spirit, the fruit of salvation, is poured out on us. As full members of the Church, we become energized, empowered — even compelled — to participate in the Church's mission to witness to this good news of our salvation.

There is a point to be stressed here. We need to regain that sense of the continuity between Good Friday, Easter Sunday, and Pentecost, just as we need to rediscover the continuity between our baptism and our confirmation. The Paschal event — God's intervention to redeem and re-create the fallen human race — embraces the full sweep of events from Good Friday through Pentecost. Our personal, sacramental participation in that saving, re-creative act embraces both baptism and confirmation. It doesn't end until we take our place at the Eucharistic table.

In summary, our catechesis regarding Pentecost should seek to make these important connections: first, the connection between the Paschal event in the Old Testament as a type of the Paschal event in the New Testament; second, as the Old Testament event embraced both the Passover-Exodus *and* the Sinai covenant, so the New Testament embraces both Jesus' death-resurrection *and* the covenanting of the disciples as the New People of God.

Send forth your Spirit. . . .

TEACHING TIPS

Transformed by the Spirit of God

Begin this activity with a simple science demonstration. Use a candle to bring a small beaker of water to a boil. Discuss how the flame transmits its heat and energy to the water, changing and energizing it in the process.

Now briefly comment how flame is one of the symbols used to describe the Spirit of God (for example, at the first Pentecost, described in Acts 2). Read the passage and explain that the Spirit transmits God's energy to us, changing and energizing us in the process.

Now have the students brainstorm some of the ways we are changed if we let God's Spirit energize us — for instance, read 1 Corinthians 13 (Love = God's Spirit). List as many of these qualities or changes as they can name, writing them on the board.

Using this list, have the students search through back copies of newsmagazines and newspapers. They are to try to find stories where one of these qualities seems to be at work: an act of kindness, forgiveness, concern, peace, etc. As they find one, discuss it as an example of the work of the Spirit, energizing and transforming society.

Variation 1: Have the students seek magazine pictures that seem to depict one or another of these qualities of God's Spirit at work in us.

Variation 2: Have the students brainstorm all the qualities associated with fire or flame: heat, warmth, light, energy, power to transform and purify.

The flickering of a flame is known to have a hypnotic, calming effect, too. Discuss all the qualities in relation to the effect the Spirit of God has on individuals and the Church at large.

In Other Words

List some of the following common expressions or make up your own:

- She has school spirit. . .
- They were filled with the spirit of Christmas. . .
- He lifted everyone's spirits. . .
- Seeing the sunset was a spiritual experience. . .
- A spirit of gloom hung over the group. . .
- She got into the spirit of the party. . .

Ask the students to come up with alternate words or phrases for "spirit" each time it occurs. In the process, explain how we often use "spirit" to decribe an invisible quality of a person or group: joy, enthusiasm, energy, etc.

Now give examples from Scripture where expressions such as "Spirit of God" or "Holy Spirit" are used. Some suggestions might include Acts 2:4, Acts 4:24-25, Acts 5:9, and Acts 8:39. You can also ask the students to hunt for other passages that refer to the Spirit. After reading a passage, discuss ways you could find a substitute expression for Spirit that would still remain true to the meaning of the passage — for example, "filled with God's courage . . . power . . . gentleness . . . wisdom." In this context introduce and explain the gifts and fruits of the Spirit.

Conclude by making the point that when God shares the gifts and fruits of his Spirit with us, God is sharing something of his own life and "personality."

This same kind of exercise can be used in helping the students form a clearer understanding of other concepts, too, including kingdom of God, Church, and faith.

Anointing Service

Using baby oil and a small amount of an inoffensive cologne, make a small bottle of chrism. This can be used in connection with various prayer services when it's appropriate to include an "anointing" service — for example, at the end of a unit to commission students to live out what they learned or at an end-of-the-year prayer service when the students are "sent forth." You can make the Sign of the Cross on the students' foreheads and/or their hands. The students can also be allowed to anoint one another. Include an appropriate prayer as the students are anointed, such as "May this oil remind you of God's Spirit who works in you." It can be very effective when done reverently.

By way of preparation, you can review the role of anointing in ancient times and its present role in celebrating the sacraments of baptism, confirmation, ordination, and the anointing of the sick.

Happy Birthday, Church!

Explain how Pentecost is the birthday of the Church. Have the students, working together or in smaller groups, discuss and then develop possible designs for a "birthday card" for the Church — symbols, appropriate saying, etc. Then have the class choose what it considers the best one. "Commission" your best class artist to prepare the card.

Now discuss how your bishop is the head of the Church in your diocese. Have all the students sign the card and send it to your bishop, as the representative of all the faithful of the diocese.

Variation: If you want to be ambitious, you could send the card to Pope John Paul II, as head of the entire Church. Who knows? You may just get a reply!

A, B, C...

This activity can be used to review a particular unit or as a "time filler." Divide the class into groups, then have them go through the alphabet, listing under each letter all the words they can think of that are related to a particular topic. For example, if your topic is Spirit of God, under *A* they might list anoint or anointing; under *B*, blessing and balm; under *F*, fire and flame. Explain that it is okay if they can't think of words for every letter.

Give a time limit, at the end of which the groups must report on their work. One group can challenge if its members feel a word isn't appropriate. If the challenged group can't defend its word adequately, it is removed. (You serve as the final judge.) The group with the most approved words for the topic "wins."

Secret Pen Pals

Provide each student with three blank envelopes. The students should write their name and summer address on the three envelopes. In each envelope they should put a slip of paper on which they write a special intention they have (perhaps for a sick parent, for help with a problem, etc.). Have the students put the envelopes containing petitions into a box you provide. Now have each student draw out three envelopes. If they get their own, they must put it back and draw again.

Stress that they should keep secret the names they draw. Now explain that they should send a little letter to each of their secret pen pals sometime during the summer, signing their name. More important, during the summer they should pray for their secret pen pal's intention when they go to Mass and at other times — like each night before bed.

You'll probably never know the effects of this activity — but be assured that good things will happen as a result.

I Still Want to Know...

Devote one of your end-of-the-year classes to this activity. In a session before the planned class, invite the students to write out questions on things "I still want to know," about the topics you studied during the year or about the Catholic faith in general. They can submit as many as they want, and they can be unsigned. Collect them and go over them before the next class, grouping similar questions, screening out the inevitable facetious ones, and preparing your answers.

In class, read each question in turn. If it is within the range of what you've been studying, invite volunteers to try to answer it. Give the "final" answer as necessary. It's a good way to find out what is on the students' minds and always makes an interesting class for everyone.

Variation: After screening the questions, you can use the "grab bag" approach described in the next activity to ensure greater class involvement. You can still provide the "final" answer.

Review: An Oldie But Goodie

Divide the students into small groups. Assign each group a chapter or topic you've studied during the year. They are to prepare five questions related to their topic. Stress that you will be using some of their questions to prepare the final test for the year. This ensures that they keep them simple and realistic.

Collect all the students' questions and put them in a paper bag. Now, by way of a contest or game, have the groups take turns drawing a question and trying to answer it. Keep score of the correct answers for each group. Continue until all the questions have been drawn. The activity is a painless way to review and gets everyone involved in a nonthreatening way.

Save the questions. Use some of the better ones when you prepare your final test.

Summer Job

Have the students discuss various ways they could help spread the Good News during the summer: acts of kindness, caring for an elderly person, giving good example by resisting peer pressures, etc. List the suggestions, trying to keep them as realistic as possible. Title the list SUMMER JOBS.

Provide each student with a blank envelope and slip of paper. The students should write their summer address on an envelope and enclose the slip on which they have written any two of the summer jobs listed.

Sometime during the summer, mail each student his or her envelope, including a short note of your own. It reminds them to try to carry out their summer jobs and affirms your interest in them.

Hawks and Doves

Have the students identify as many realistic "hawk" situations as they can in which they have experienced strife and fighting in their lives. Some possible examples might include fighting with a brother or sister over whose turn it is to clean up the kitchen, name-calling and fighting with a rival school, and arguments on the playground.

Divide the class into small groups, then give all of the groups one of the problem situations identified. It should be the same situation for all groups. Now explain briefly that the Spirit of God is often symbolized as a dove because the Spirit brings peace and gentleness into our lives.

Have the groups then discuss and try to come up with a creative "dove" solution for either preventing or resolving the "hawk" situation. Have the groups share their ideas with one another. The group with the best idea is given the DOVE AWARD FOR THE WEEK. Repeat the activity periodically. Or use it when a "hawk" situation actually arises in the class or school, reminding the students to seek help from the Holy Spirit whenever they face a difficult problem.

Open the Doors

Explain that the Spirit is closed out of our lives and can't guide us when there is excessive noise present. Explain that there are basically two kinds of noise:

• *Physical noise* — always having the radio or TV blaring keeps us from hearing the Spirit.

• *Emotional noise* — anger, fear, resentment, etc., drive out the Spirit.

Now suggest that the students take some time each day to be quiet — physically and emotionally — so that they can open the door for the Spirit to come into their hearts.

To get them started in this practice, consider spending three to five minutes in silence and reflection at the beginning or at some appropriate time in the middle of the next few classes. You'll be amazed to find that most students actually enjoy this exercise in silence. Then help them name and decide upon some time during their routine day when they can "practice silence" on their own. Remind them about this for the next few classes. You'll be doing them — and the Spirit — a big favor by helping them cultivate this practice.

Chapter 9
The Church and the Laity

As catechists, one of our ongoing tasks is to unfold the multifaceted mystery of the Church for our children, not just intellectually but experientially. The Church is not "a truth" to be memorized. It is a living, dynamic reality in which we are called to consciously participate. Admittedly, this is a challenge.

The following model, adapted from the work of Avery Dulles, S.J., can serve as a tool for organizing your catechesis. It looks something like this:

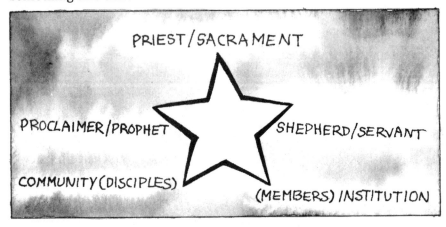

In this model, the bottom terms describe the *who* the Church is and *how* it is organized. We are a community of disciples, persons bound to Jesus and to one another by the universal bonds of faith and love. At the same time, we are members of a visible institution, bound together by a visible head, by a common Creed and by clearly stated obligations.

Certain scriptural images reflect the communal nature of the Church: People of God, for example, or Bride of Christ. They suggest intimacy, personal warmth, and familial spontaneity. Certain scriptural images reflect the institutional nature of the Church — for instance, Temple of God, the New Jerusalem. They suggest visible, tangible qualities of strength, order, and symmetry.

These two "organizational" aspects of the nature of the Church exist in a creative tension. The vitality of the Church as a community of disciples continually requires the discipline and order of the Church as an institution or it would disintegrate into subjective, relativized splinter sects. This was the threat posed by the Protestant Reformation in the sixteenth century. On the other hand, the Church as an institution continually needs the intangible, humanizing qualities of love, joy, compassion, spontaneity, and personal charisms or it would evolve into an oppressive, self-serving religion of the kind promoted by the Pharisees in Jesus' time.

In the short view, one or another of these two "organizational" concepts of the Church seems to be more popular or more right for the times. Again, in the short view, we may personally find one or more appealing while other Catholics prefer the other. But in the long view we need both, and throughout history they continually serve as self-correcting forces within the Church. What often appears to be conflict in the short view is actually a sign of this creative tension that must always exist between these two essential aspects of the Church's nature.

In terms of our own catechesis, then, we need to be careful to maintain this balance. Certainly we can stress one aspect at one point of the children's development and the other aspect at another stage. For example, the communal aspect of the Church is more easily grasped by small children and is usually more appealing to adolescents. The institutional aspect can often be most effectively presented to the logical minds of the middle grade and junior high youth. In our overall program, though, and at each stage in our program, we need to strive for balance. We especially need to guard against allowing our own personal biases and preferences to keep us from presenting this balanced view. A balanced catechesis will give our children a solid foundation upon which to build their understanding of the mystery which is the Church. It will also help the students see the inevitable creative conflict within the Church in a positive rather than a negative light.

Now, let's look at the top three elements in the model. They describe the threefold ministry of Jesus as prophet, priest, and shepherd. They also define the Church in terms of *what* it does. As such they allow us to unfold for the children the various facets of the ministering Church. Whether we talk of the Church as a community or as an institution, it will be involved in the same ministries. Clearly, these ministries are interdependent and mutually supportive, not competitive. At the same time, one can take precedence over another in a given situation. Some situations call for healing and reconciliation; others call for prophetic confrontation; some call for patient teaching; and still others demand a response of worship and celebration.

Also, in this model it becomes clear that all ministry will need both communal concern and institutional discipline to be effective and to endure. At times, ministry will call for sacramentally ordained, officially recognized and properly trained ministers. And it will need to be guided by officially approved methods. At the same time, ministry should not become bureaucratic, impersonal, and impeded by excessive formalism or legalism of the kind Jesus often encountered.

Ideally, the best way to help children understand the Church in terms of *what* it does is by providing them with experiences of the ministering Church and when they are old enough, by providing them with opportunities to participate in ministry. In our classroom catechesis, though, let our goal again be balance: to introduce the children to the variety and richness of the Church's nature as manifest in its call to participate in the threefold ministry of Jesus.

In the final analysis, the Church remains a mystery. No single definition, model, or image can capture the depth and breadth of its nature. That's why Scripture itself abounds in various images, as so many facets of the same diamond. The Church is the Bride of Christ, the People of God, a Priestly People, the New Jerusalem, the Temple of God, the Body of Christ, Sacrament, Vine and Branches.

In summary, let these few norms guide your catechesis. (1) Taking this cue from Scripture itself, do not become too dependent on any one model or image in seeking to present the Church to our children. (2) Remain willing to adapt your choice of images and models to the readiness of the children. (3) Continually seek to maintain a balanced view yourself. (4) Finally, seek to include, in your teaching about the Church, opportunities to experience the living Church in one or another of its dimensions.

And as in all your catechetical efforts, leave some room for the Holy Spirit.

THEOLOGY UPDATE

'Democracy in the Church'

The Synod on the Laity finished its work on October 30, 1987. But certain tensions between the clergy and the laity remain. These tensions don't have their roots in theological questions about the dignity, responsibilities, and mission of the laity, questions of major concern for the synod. The tensions are rooted in an often unspoken issue of power.

Put simply, the issue is this: Who is in charge? Is the Church a monarchy with the pope as king or is it a democracy where baptism gives each person an equal vote? How one answers these questions is critical. If the Church is a monarchy ruled over by the pope — and by extension the local bishops and ultimately the local pastor — then the clergy still hold all the power. On the other hand, if the Church is a democracy, then the laity have the power because they make up the majority within the Church.

Though the question is real in the minds of many, clergy and laity alike, neither of the above "answers" is correct. The only correct answer is that the Church in essence is neither a monarchy nor a democracy. The Church in its essence is *governed by the Spirit through the charisms bestowed on its members.*

The charism for preserving and explaining the revelation entrusted to the community was first bestowed on the Apostles and then in an unbroken chain upon their successors. This particular charism and consequent responsibility for officially guiding, teaching, and protecting the Church from error now resides with the pope in union with the other bishops. This *irrefutable* theological fact, however, does not make the Church a monarchy. Nor does it prevent the principles of democracy from being applied to the Church.

Monarchy and democracy are human inventions and both suffer from human limitations. The theoretical benefits and weaknesses of each have been the topic of philosophic debate from Plato onward. That the Church, understood as an institution, does employ a monarchical model today is more a historical "accident" than a revealed and therefore theological necessity. Perhaps, had Jesus first entered history in twentieth-century Western civilization rather than the first century in the Middle East, some form of the democratic model would have been adopted by the institutional Church.

A majority vote, however, can never remove the charisms and consequent authority for maintaining orthodoxy bestowed by the Spirit on the pope and bishops. If that were the case, we would all be Arians today, because at the time of the Council of Nicaea the majority of Christians, including many of the bishops, had embraced that heresy. The charism for maintaining orthodoxy and the practical implications of the charism for the governance of the Church is above both monarchical and democratic models of governing. It is rooted in and sustained by the Spirit who ultimately governs the Church.

Having said this, what practical roles does this distinction have for reducing the tensions we described above? Simply this: The *exercise* of this critical charism of governance can be carried out in either a monarchical or a democratic way. In countries like our own where the laity are both theologically literate and also culturally conditioned to use the tools of the democratic process — dialogue, consultation, the formation of a consensus, and more recently discernment — the democratic model can work very well. This fact was dramatically proven by the process used by the United States bishops in developing their pastoral on the economy. They sought — and took very seriously — the expertise and the opinions of the entire faith community. That process of gathering and respecting the "public wisdom" is at the very heart of the democratic process. But we must be clear on this fact: Employing such a democratic process in no way diminishes the bishops' (or the pope's) unique apostolic charism and responsibility to teach authoritatively. Rather, it enhances it by utilizing the various other charisms — given by the same Spirit — that are present throughout the faith community.

This "democratic" process is admittedly cumbersome. It is not always reasonable to expect it to work "worldwide." In countries where people are not culturally conditioned to function in a democratic way it might even be harmful. But, in those countries like our own, what the "democratic process" loses in efficiency it gains in the community's understanding of and receptivity to the authoritative directives and decisions of the hierarchy that result.

So the bottom line is this: All of us, laity and clergy alike, would be wiser if we stopped seeking an either-or solution to how the institutional Church should be governed. It is governed by the Spirit through the charisms bestowed on the Church. Having agreed to that, the laity and the clergy in a parish can then work together to find the best way for those charisms to be exercised in their particular circumstances. Our own cultural bias suggests that democratic processes can usually enhance the exercise of the charisms. But this may not be true in other parts of the world — or in particular parishes in our own country. Under certain conditions a "benevolent dictatorship" can actually be the most effective model, provided it is both solicited and supported by the "governed."

"But one and the same Spirit produces all of these, distributing them individually to each person as he wishes" (1 Corinthians 12:11).

TEACHING TIPS

A Star Is Born

Use the image of the star presented in the CATECHETICAL REFLECTION section to explain the various dimensions or aspects of the Church: Priest/Sacrament, Proclaimer/Prophet, Shepherd/Servant, Community (Disciples), (Members) Institution.

Spend as much time as necessary to explain the Church in this way. After the students have a basic understanding of each dimension, have them draw a large star on a piece of poster board. They should cut out the star, then in each point of the star they should paste in — collage fashion — appropriate pictures and words from old magazines that depict that aspect of the Church. You may prefer to have small groups of students do a star together as a group project. Display the completed stars around the room.

Variation 1: Have the students bring in medium-size cardboard boxes and instruct them to cover the boxes with white butcher paper, except for the bottom side. The five sides of the box now represent the five different aspects of the Church. Again, have the students do collages on all five sides. Make a display of the finished boxes for the back of the church or the school hall.

Variation 2: On the board make five columns, each titled by one of the aspects of the Church. Brainstorm with the students to come up with as many local parish activities and organizations as possible. As each is named, have the students help you decide under which column that activity or organization belongs.

Variation 3: Have the students make mobiles using coat hangers, string, and five pieces of colored cardboard. Each piece of cardboard should be designed or decorated in such a way as to represent one of the dimensions of the Church.

With a Song in My Heart

For this activity you'll need some copies of Sunday missalettes or hymnbooks. Divide the class into groups of four to five students each. Each group should find a hymn with which they are familiar. Or, if you prefer, you may help the whole class choose one hymn. In either case, the small groups must now write new lyrics that will fit the melody of the hymn — *on the theme of Church*. The new hymns should consist of a chorus and two verses. This presupposes that you have already spent some time studying the nature of the Church.

When the groups are finished, each group should read or sing its lyrics to the class. If you have the ability, you can help them sing or accompany them in some other way. After each song is presented, ask the class to evaluate it in terms of its ''theology.'' This is a fun way to deal with an otherwise difficult and sometimes boring subject. If possible, arrange to use the songs in the following weeks in class prayer services.

You can use this approach with just about any other religious topic, too. This kind of paraphrasing is within the ability of the students, especially when working as a group.

'Catholic High Five'

As a filler sometime, try this. Explain to the students how the early Christians would greet one another with the expression ''Shalom'' and with a kiss of peace. Relate this to the various special ''handshakes'' used by athletes and others today. Then challenge the students to come up with their own version of a ''Catholic high five'' for today's Church. You'll be amused by what they come up with. Encourage them to use their new handshake. It's a harmless and simple way to help build a sense of Christian identity.

Who, What, When, and Where?

Here is a challenging way to teach older students about Easter. Give them the following passages in the New Testament: Matthew 27:57—28:20; Mark 16:1-19; Luke 24:1-52; John 20:1-23.

These are the passages that describe the events surrounding Jesus' resurrection on the first Easter Sunday. Invite the students, working alone or in small groups, to be detectives. They should try to come up with a step-by-step ''police report'' of these events in the order in which they occurred. Each evangelist is a different witness they interview. These witnesses sometimes give apparently conflicting testimony. Sifting through the testimony, they must come up with what they think is the most accurate version. They should list each event, who was involved, what happened, where it happened, and the approximate time it happened.

The groups should then share their reports and attempt to defend them to the class. We guarantee a lively session. It will also generate a lot of interest in the events themselves — which is the real purpose.

St. Joseph — The Forgotten Saint

St. Joseph is the husband of Mary and was chosen from all eternity to nurture, educate, and protect the child Jesus together with her. Because of his role in our redemption, Joseph is the patron of the universal Church and second only to Mary in terms of the honor the Church bestows on him. Traditionally, his feast was celebrated on March 19 and March was traditionally dedicated to devotion to Joseph. Using his litany (it can be found in most older missals and prayer books), introduce your class to the titles and qualities of this "forgotten saint." Joseph in the Old Testament is considered a type of St. Joseph. The expression "Go to Joseph," as found in the Old Testament, is now the motto for St. Joseph as our universal patron. Teach your students this motto during March.

Scripture Search

You can approach this activity in one of two ways. You can personally identify fifteen or twenty New Testament passages for the students to look up and then classify. That is, they should indicate which dimension of the Church the passage refers to (as described in the CATECHETICAL REFLECTION) — for example, Matthew 16:16-20 would be listed under Institution, Acts 2:42-47 would be listed under Community, Mark 1:23-38 would refer to Shepherd/Servant.

Or you may prefer to explain the project and have the students skim through the Gospels, seeking a given number of passages to put under each of the five categories.

With either approach, the students will begin to see the scriptural roots for our understanding of the Church. You will also have a means for measuring if the students are forming a clear understanding of each of the dimensions of the Church.

Little-Known Facts

Using the *Catholic Almanac* (published by Our Sunday Visitor), the Maryknoll *Catholic Dictionary*, or any reputable Church history book, gather "trivia" about the Church and Church history; some possible examples might include a diocese used to refer to the districts into which the Roman Empire was divided; over five million Christians died in the Roman persecutions; Vatican City is actually a sovereign country, the smallest in the world; before 1918, a person did not have to be a priest to be a cardinal.

Post two or three of these a week on a special bulletin board in the form of questions — for instance, "Where do we get the word 'diocese'?" or "How many Christians died during the Roman persecutions?'' Encourage the students to try to find the answers for extra credit. Give the answers the following week and post new questions.

You'll be surprised at the amount of interest this little activity can generate — and how much information you can share in a painless way.

Parish Honor Roll

Make a large poster on which you list all the various parish organizations that are operative in which laity play a major role: parish council, board of education, altar society, St. Vincent de Paul Society, CCD program, lectors, Communion distributors, servers, choir/musicians, ushers, hospitality committee, ministry to shut-ins, etc. Don't list the names of persons, just names of organizations and ministries. Be as complete as you can. You may wish to involve the students in doing the research necessary to compile this list.

Letter and decorate the poster as artistically as you can (or have the students make the poster). Title it PARISH HONOR ROLL or perhaps LAITY IN MINISTRY. Each week take a few minutes in class to describe one of the ministries listed, the work performed, and the importance of the work.

Variation 1: Each week assign a different student the task of preparing a three-minute report on a particular ministry.

Variation 2: Whenever possible, invite an actual member of that ministry to visit the class, give a short description of the ministry, and answer questions.

Parish Scrapbook

Purchase or, with the help of your students, make a scrapbook. Designate several pages for each of the corporal and spiritual works of mercy. Make individual students or small groups of students responsible for lettering the title page for each of the works: Group One is responsible for ''Feed the Hungry,'' Group Two is responsible for ''Clothe the Naked,'' etc. They can also decorate their title page with drawings, appropriate pictures, and so forth.

Keep the completed book available in some prominent place in the classroom. Now alert the class to be on the lookout for events and activities in the parish that relate to one or another of these works of mercy: Thanksgiving food drive, mission collection, funerals and wake services, etc. Each time the students become aware of such an activity (done by a group or an individual) they should report it to the class and then record it in the scrapbook.

Encourage the students, alone or in groups, to undertake certain works of their own and then record these also.

Variation: Rather than restricting the scrapbook to parish activities, you may want to have the students scan newspapers for the presence of these works in society in general.

Membership Card

Discuss with the students what it means for them to be members of the Church. Stress especially the significance of their baptism and how this initiation gives them a share in Jesus' ministry as priest, teacher/prophet and shepherd/servant.

As a class, now discuss together the design of a "membership card" the students could make that would reflect the meaning of their membership in the Church. You can start with membership cards they already have, such as from the Boy or Girl Scouts, to get some initial ideas. As an alternative, have each student submit a sample card and then combine the best ideas into a single "class card." Have your most artistic student then produce a master. Make copies on a hard cardboard for the students to carry with them.

Variation: Rather than make a Church membership card have the students do the same activity for parish membership.

'Family' Shield

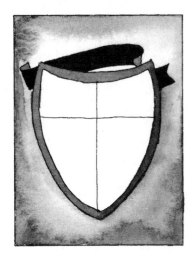

Invite the students, working alone or in small groups, to design a shield or family crest for the Church. First discuss together the main vocations or roles within the Church: marriage, priesthood, single life, religious life. Then discuss various ministries in the Church: teaching, healing, leadership, and so forth. After sufficient discussion have the students design shields or crests that depict these vocations and ministries. Provide poster paper, Magic Markers, colored paper, scissors, and paste.

Have a "show and tell" when the projects are completed and then display all the shields around the room.

Variation: Do the same project, but make your parish the subject of the shield.

Board Charades

Divide the class into two groups. Give each group a set of 3" x 5" cards on which you have written words or phrases related to your topic. But keep the words as abstract as possible — for example, ministry, laity, service, community, domestic church. Team One picks its representative. Team Two gives the representative one of its cards. The representative goes to the board and attempts to "draw" some symbol or other depiction of the word or phrase on the card. Members of Team One try to guess the word or phrase, a la the game Charades. If they guess it after the first picture, the team gets two points. If they can't guess the word, the representative is allowed to draw a second "picture." If the team gets it after the second "picture," it gets one point. If it still doesn't guess it, Team Two gets a point. Then Team Two picks a representative and Team One selects one of its cards. Continue until all cards are used or until time is up.

A variation that will involve the whole class is as follows:

Ask for one person to volunteer to be the "guesser" and another to be the "drawer." Both go to the front of the room. You give the "drawer" a word or phrase to depict — and show the word to everyone else except the "guesser." The "drawer" goes to the board and is given one chance to depict the word. If the "guesser" doesn't get it, call on another volunteer to attempt a drawing. Continue calling on volunteers until the "guesser" discovers the phrase. The person who successfully depicted the word now becomes the "guesser" and the game continues. This can be a good way to review any topic you are studying. It really challenges the students to use their imagination and to make abstract concepts more tangible.

The "drawers" can break the word down into syllables with a "picture" for each syllable. They can also do "sounds like" pictures (for example, minister = mini + stir).

Birthday List

If you have a number of shut-ins in your parish or if there is a retirement home nearby, try this.

Obtain the birthdays of five or ten people you wish to show concern for. Then find out from the nursing staff or relatives small items of special interest to these elderly persons: special fruit, a favorite magazine, bath powder, etc. Make it a class project to assemble a "care package" to deliver to each person on your list on his or her birthday. Different groups of students can take turns making these deliveries.

Funds to purchase these small items can be obtained by student donations or by small fund-raising projects. A card, made and signed by the students, can accompany the care package. It's a good way to keep the spirit of concern and giving alive all through the year.

Thank-you Notes

Near Thanksgiving, put all the students' names on envelopes and have each student draw out an envelope. Stress to the students that they should allow no one to see the name on their envelope. The students should now write a brief "thank-you note" to the student whose name they drew, expressing at least one thing that student does to help make the class a better place. They should not sign the note. Collect the envelopes when the students are finished, by having them place the envelopes in a box. Pass out the envelopes to the students whose names are on them and allow them time to read the notes. End the session with a short Thanksgiving prayer service around the theme of gratefulness for one another.

Chapter 10
Discipleship and Vocations

The process of discerning a vocation is not unlike the party game Treasure Hunt. Participants receive a starting clue. Using it they proceed to find new clues, each leading them closer to the final clue that reveals the treasure. Granting weaknesses in the comparison, vocations do tend to unfold one clue at a time. Each clue points in the direction to be taken next. It isn't always easy to interpret the clues. There can be false starts that lead us in the wrong direction. But with help and perseverance our vocation, like the treasure, becomes clear to us.

The clues God plants for each child include his or her personal talents, gifts, natural attractions, and interests. They include the circumstances of life, family influence, and the influence of teachers, friends, and associates. They also include awareness of the needs of the Church and the direct invitations to serve the Church.

Viewed superficially such clues are quite commonplace and natural. Viewed with the larger perspective of faith, each is a personal grace to the child manifesting Christ's call to personal friendship and to special service in his name. As catechists our task is to help the children recognize and respond to the clues — that is, the graces by which God is calling each of them. We can do this in several ways:

1. We can do this in a personal way by helping our children recognize and appreciate the unique talents, interests, and aptitudes with which they are gifted.

2. We can do this in a more general way by presenting and explaining the needs of the Church in our time and by teaching that each of us, according to our talent, is being called to share in the mission of the Church.

3. We can do this formally by teaching the children factual

information about the traditional vocations within the Church: marriage, single state, priesthood, and brotherhood and sisterhood in religious community.

4. We can do this experientially by providing the children with opportunities to meet people in the various vocations and allowing them to become familiar with the lifestyle and ministry of each.

5. We can do this in an ongoing way by encouraging the children to continually pray for guidance in interpreting the clues through which Jesus is calling them to serve him.

6. Finally, and perhaps most important, we can directly invite the individual students to begin to seriously consider a particular vocation for which they manifest the aptitude and qualifications.

None of the above approaches are particularly dramatic and need not be. Elementary school is a time to lay foundations and plant seeds, not reap the harvest. But elementary school remains an ideal time to promote in the children an awareness that each is being called personally by Jesus to be co-workers with him in some special way.

That is the bottom line in all catechesis regarding vocations. By our birth into this world and by our rebirth at baptism we are called forth by God to serve him. Children still have years ahead of them for discerning what unique role God has for them. But from early childhood onward it is important to nurture in them the awareness that they are being called. Through our catechesis and through our ongoing personal relationship with the children, we have ample opportunity to nurture this awareness. God has planted the clues. Our task is to heighten the children's alertness in looking for them. Or to use another more biblical image, God has already planted the seeds of vocation in each child. Our task is to water and cultivate.

THEOLOGY UPDATE

Vocations

In seeking to better understand the concept of vocation, some distinctions can be helpful. First, we can speak of vocation in the biblical and theological sense. Second, there is vocation in the historical and cultural sense.

In the biblical and theological sense vocation is intimately linked to the concept of name and the act of naming. (In Hebrew, "to call" and "to name" have the same etymology.) "To name" is related to the act of creation itself and as such is properly the prerogative of God, the Creator of all things. When God invited Adam to name the animals, he was bestowing God-like dignity on humanity, clearly setting us apart from the lower animals. In the biblical context, one's name reveals the person's unique role and destiny within the community and within God's plan of salvation. That is the significance of God's intervention to change Abram's name to

Abraham or Jacob's name to Israel. God personally chooses the name for John the Baptizer and, of course, for Jesus.

Likewise Scripture tells us that God calls each person by name and that he has our names written on the palm of his hand. Our unique, most inner self is intimately known by God our Creator. He has a special, unique role for each of us just as he did for Abraham, Israel, John, and Paul. Our vocation may not seem so dramatic or be so dramatically revealed, but it is just as real. God has a role for us in his plan of salvation and he remains intimately involved in helping us discover and fulfill that role.

Thus, in the biblical and theological sense each of us has a unique potential that is intrinsically related to being created by God. It is contained in the "name" by which God has called us forth from nothingness into existence and from spiritual death to rebirth in baptism. In this sense each of us has the unique vocational task of discovering the name by which God calls us and of achieving the potential it signifies.

In the historical and cultural sense our unique vocation is lived out within one of the four traditional states of life within the Church: marriage, the single state, religious life, or the priesthood. Each of these states is important to the life of the Church, of course. At various points in history one or another has had a larger role to play. For example, hermits played important roles in deepening the Church's spiritual life in the fourth and fifth centuries. The great monastic orders and then the great mendicant orders shaped the conscience of the Church in the Middle Ages. Great teaching and missionary communities assumed a central role after the Reformation. Marriage and priesthood, of course, have remained essential vocations throughout all ages of the Church's life.

In our times there is talk of a vocation crisis. More properly we are confronted with significant cultural upheaval in society and consequently within the Church itself. The distinct roles for priests, religious, married couples, and single persons are tending to blur and overlap. Some forms of religious life and monastic life are fading. New forms are emerging. The proper responsibilities of priests and laity are being redefined. Hence, as young people face vocational decisions in terms of choosing a particular state in life, the choices aren't quite as clear-cut as in the past. Ministry is not the exclusive responsibility or prerogative of priests and religious as it once seemed to be. In our time, it seems more proper to talk of a cultural and historical evolution in vocations rather than a crisis in vocations.

In any event, each of us has a unique vocation within God's plan of salvation, bestowed on us with the name by which God calls us into existence. This unique vocation will be lived out within one of the four general states of life (vocations) that have traditionally been part of the Church's makeup. While the precise nature, roles, and responsibilities of these vocations are to some degree in a state of flux, each will endure as an essential part of the Church's life. Each will remain an essential way to respond to Christ's call to his Church to share with him in building the kingdom and caring for his people.

TEACHING TIPS

The Five P's

List the five qualities of discipleship on the board: personal, permanent (loyal), participative, prayerful, and patient. Explain each of the qualities and give examples.

Option One: Divide the class into five groups. Provide poster paper, old magazines, glue, and Magic Markers. Instruct each group to create a poster reflecting the elements of the particular discipleship-quality they chose. When each group is finished, create a mural by putting all the posters side by side on one wall.

Option Two: Divide the class into five groups and assign each group one of the disciple-qualities, as in Option One. Instruct each group to discuss and then list at least five ways people their age can exercise that particular quality of discipleship. Have the groups share their ideas with the total class, and then have the class pick the best idea from each group. List these five ideas on a poster board and display it. Remind the students that they should occasionally try to carry out the ideas they have identified.

Option Three: Form the class into groups and assign the discipleship-qualities as in Options One and Two. Ask each group to develop bumper-sticker-type sayings related to their assigned quality (or to discipleship in general). For example: "Disciples are people persons" and "Disciples don't give up." Have the groups share their sayings with the whole class, and then have the class choose the best ones. If you like, you can have the students actually make bumper stickers by using plain white contact paper.

Variation: Using the same approach, have the students make buttons instead of bumper stickers.

Help Wanted

Take examples of help-wanted ads from the local newspaper and review them with the class. Then instruct each student to compose a similar help-wanted ad of the kind Jesus might have put in the paper in seeking disciples.

Invite volunteers to share their work with the class.

Variation: For older students, you can add some challenge by limiting them to twenty-five words.

Come, Follow Me

Put the following headings on the chalkboard (or overhead projector):

DISCIPLESHIP

Costs   *Rewards*   *Obstacles*

Brainstorm with the students, seeking their ideas for each of the three categories. Encourage them to give suggestions appropriate for their age-group. For example, "Fear of teasing" might be an obstacle they face. A cost might be "Having to give up TV time to help out little brother or sister." Discuss the completed list together and help the class come up with a definition of discipleship that would apply to people their age.

Living Examples

Obtain a list of names and phone numbers of persons who are engaged in various ministries in your parish. Here is a sample list to work from:

- Lector(s).
- Eucharistic minister(s).
- Deacon.
- CCD teacher(s).
- Pastoral visitor(s).
- St. Vincent de Paul Society.
- Parish council.
- Music director.
- Baptismal couple(s).
- Marriage preparation couple(s).
- Social concerns committee.
- Altar Society member(s).

Assign each student one person to interview by phone or in person. Provide this or a similar list of questions the students are to ask:

- Why did you get involved in this ministry?
- Did you need any special training?
- Do you get any personal benefits from your work?
- How did you first decide to get involved: Who invited you?
- Do you think it is a good idea for everyone to get involved in some form of ministry: Why or why not?

Based on the answers they receive, students are to prepare a short written or oral report on their interviews. When these are shared with the class, ask the class to listen for any common themes about ministry and discipleship that emerge. For example, common benefits reported, how most people first become involved, etc. Discuss with the class the common themes they noted.

To make this activity a good experience for everyone involved, it is a good idea to let the people on your list know ahead of time that your students will be contacting them.

Variation: Invite a representative from each of the various ministries in your parish to visit your class and give a short explanation of what their particular ministry is about. You can give these representatives the questions listed above as a guide to help them prepare their little talk.

Saint — Disciple

Assign individuals or small groups a particular saint to research. Have them prepare a written report, an oral report, or a poster that identifies ways their particular saint demonstrated the various qualities of discipleship.

Variation: This activity can be spread throughout the year. Assign your students various saints whose feasts will be celebrated during the school year. Have the students give their reports to the class on or near the saint's feast day.

Mail Call

Often it is not possible to arrange for different priests and religious to talk to the students about their vocation. Here is a good substitute. Obtain names and addresses of individuals in various vocations in your church. Such a list might include a teaching brother and sister, health-care ministers, missionaries, diocesan priest, or a member of a contemplative order. If possible, identify persons from the parish in any of these vocations.

Help the students compose a letter to each person identified. In the letter they should ask several basic questions:

- Can you describe a typical day in your life?
- What helped you decide you had a vocation to this kind of life?
- What qualities should a person have who is thinking about a vocation like yours?

Include in the letter a request for a personal snapshot, if possible. After you have received the return letters, read and discuss them together. Then make a poster with the letter and snapshot of each person. Add a reminder to pray for vocations. Display the posters around the school.

Hall of Fame

If there have been a number of religious or priestly vocations from your parish over the years, have the students develop a bulletin board display of these people. Families of the priests or religious can help provide pictures, dates, and other information. Arrange to display the completed project in the back of the church or in some prominent location in the school.

Help Wanted

This is a popular activity and is always fun. After studying together the various vocations (active/contemplative, priest/religious, missionary, teacher, health care, service to the poor, etc.), direct the students to compose "help wanted" ads for each vocation. Provide samples of help-wanted ads from the local newspaper to give them an idea of the format to use.

Finished products can be reproduced as posters and displayed around the school.

God's Call

Have the students use their Bibles to find the passages that depict God's call to some of the following:

- Abram, later renamed Abraham by God (Genesis 12:1-4).
- Moses (Exodus 3:1-6, 9-12, and 4:10-17).
- Aaron (Exodus 4:27-31).
- Samuel (1 Samuel 3:1-10).

- Elijah (1 Kings 19:9-21).
- Isaiah (Isaiah 6:1-13).
- Jeremiah (Jeremiah 1:4-10).
- Ezekiel (Ezekiel 2:1 to 3:9).
- Mary (Luke 1:26-38).
- The Apostles (Matthew 4:18-25).
- Saul, or Paul (Acts 9:1-19).
- The Rich Young Man (Luke 18:18-25).

After the students read these passages, direct them to identify any common elements in some of the calls. For example, several people were very surprised; others resisted initially.

In light of the discussion explain the fact that most people don't experience the kind of direct calls depicted in Scripture. Now discuss ways God can issue the call today that are less direct than the Scripture calls.

Scrapbook

This extended project can be very educational. Identify a representative list of various religious communities. Give special attention to those working in your diocese. Using *The Official Catholic Directory* or advertisements in religious magazines to obtain addresses, direct the students to write to these communities to obtain the following information:

1. Who founded the community? When? Where?

2. What are the primary ministries of the community?

3. What are the present numbers and in what places do members work?

4. What are the requirements for membership? Length and kind of training?

5. Are there any saints or other famous members from the community's history?

Most communities have brochures containing this kind of information and are eager to share them. After material is gathered, the students in groups should prepare a page or more of information on each community to be inserted in a scrapbook. Provide the students with a common format for making their reports for the scrapbook, including space to attach brochures, pictures, etc.

Variation: Using the same approach have each group prepare a separate folder for each community.

Keep the scrapbook or folder file available in class for perusal by the students during free time or "donate" it to the school library, making it available to other teachers and classes.

Day by Day

The calendar of saints each month gives a rich tapestry of the variety of ways people have responded to God's call. Each month assign several students the task to research one or more saints whose feast is celebrated that month. Choose saints for variety as much as possible.

Have the students give a report on the saint's accomplishments, talents, and trials. In the context of these reports remind the class that all of us have talents and are being called to be saints regardless of the state of life to which we are called.

Variation: Each student can prepare such a report for his or her saint, on that saint's feast day or on the child's birthday. Use the report as an occasion to remind the students of their own call to sanctity and to God's service.

Job, Career, Vocation

You can use St. Paul's life as a good basis for helping children understand the difference between a job, a career, and a vocation.

1. Paul occasionally worked as a tentmaker to support himself. Jobs are things we primarily do for the money we need.

2. Paul's talents lay in teaching, preaching, and leadership. A career is the kind of work to which we are attracted because of special talents and interests. Money received, though important, is not the primary reason for pursuing a career.

3. Paul received a special call to be the Apostle to the Gentiles. A vocation is God's special plan for us. It may or may not be directly tied to our job or career.

Stress the point that jobs and careers may change several times during one's lifetime. The vocation to be a saint, however, and to fulfill God's plan for us remains constant regardless of those changes.

Prayer Contest

A good way to review and summarize a series of lessons on the topic of vocations is to direct each student to compose a short prayer for vocations.

Allow the class to then listen to and judge the prayers, choosing the three that best seem to express the ideas of vocation that were presented in the lessons. Use the chosen prayers on a rotating basis to begin or end your class periodically.

Variation: Assign groups of students a different specific vocation for which to compose a prayer. For example, married couples, single persons, male and female religious, diocesan and religious priests.

Chapter 11
Morality and Conscience Formation

CATECHETICAL REFLECTION

An integral goal of our catechesis is to assist parents and the overall Christian community in the task of nurturing a Christ-like conscience in the children we teach. Sometimes we will do this directly — for example, when we deal with a specific moral topic like the Ten Commandments. More often we will do this indirectly. Let's review briefly what is involved in the formation of conscience in order to identify ways of helping the children "put on the mind of Christ."

The ancient philosophers rooted morality in the golden rule: Treat others as you would have them treat you. Jesus did as much when he cited the second "great" commandment as the duty to love others as we love ourselves. St. Paul tells us that each of us is born with the law of God written in our heart. There is a common thread here. From early childhood onward, each of us has a basic awareness of what is good for us. We know our own "rights." For example, we want others to tell us the truth, not lies. Even small children object when they discover that they have been lied to. We sense that we have a basic right to physical well-being and consider ourselves wronged if others seek to do us physical harm. It is the same with the right to property, reputation, and so forth.

Therefore, conscience is rooted in our inner awareness of what is good for us, an awareness that is "written in our hearts." A maturing conscience is one that expands and begins to recognize and respect the *same rights in others*. Even at the level of unaided reason, we are capable of making rather noble decisions by asking this simple question: How would I like to be treated in this situation? The answer tells how I should then treat my neighbor.

The practical implication in catechesis is that we should continually challenge children to ask that question: "How would I like to be treated in this situation?'' In this process, we should help them develop a sensitivity to the fact that others have the *same* rights, needs, and aspirations as ourselves. This ability to make ''moral transference'' is basic to moral development. Fortunately, even children can begin to make this transference and recognize the reasonableness and fairness of the ''laws'' that flow from the golden rule.

Unfortunately, things are not always quite this neat. Another dimension of conscience formation is rooted, not in our hearts, but in the family and circumstances in which we grow. These influences complicate our formation and can be negative forces that distort the kind of innate moral reasoning just described. One kind of distortion can be labeled ''tribalism.'' From the time they are little onward, children can be taught to ignore the claim to equal rights for certain kinds of people. A classic example is how children of slave owners in pre-Civil War America were frequently taught to regard slaves. The ''equal rights'' principle simply did not apply to blacks. Slaves were an exception to the golden rule. We can only wonder about children growing up amid the conflict and hatred of Northern Ireland or Lebanon or in the poverty of Haiti. How easy does it become for them to hate certain groups of people and disregard their claim to ''equal rights''? And feel morally correct in doing so? Closer to home, we have less dramatic examples of the kind of distortion a culture can inflict on children. Many adults who otherwise consider lying wrong do not regard cheating on tests (or on income-tax forms), for example, to be lying. In the same way, some do not regard shoplifting as stealing.

When these kinds of distortions are present in the family or in a society, children readily begin to fit them into their moral reasoning. Their consciences become malformed, but they do not have the slightest idea that their moral reasoning is defective. As catechists, it is good for us to remember that conscience can be so easily silenced or distorted. That way, we will better appreciate our role in the formation of conscience. As catechists, we need to be alert to signs of these kinds of defects in the moral reasoning of the children. Remember, children are usually unaware that there is anything wrong with their thinking. They are sincerely imitating the example around them. So the task is to challenge the symptoms of ''tribalism'' and other distortions by clearly pointing out the errors. In short, we need to help the children recognize and be able to label deeds and attitudes that are wrong, both in themselves and in others.

Finally, our conscience is shaped by faith. Faith transforms rather than distorts our natural moral reasoning. Faith reveals to us truth about ourselves and others that reason alone cannot provide. Faith here is taken to mean both the personal recognition of Jesus Christ as our Lord and Savior, and the acceptance of the beliefs and teachings of the Church. Faith, in this sense, becomes an objective standard against which we measure our own behavior. Faith allows us to judge whether our actions are right or wrong, good or evil.

Central to a faith-grounded conscience is the fact that Jesus taught that we are the very children of God! This sense of our God-like dignity gives a radical new meaning to "what is good for us" and how we should love ourselves. By extension, it gives a whole new meaning to the golden rule, the respect we should have for our neighbor and their rights as children of God. Jesus goes further and teaches that *everyone* is our neighbor, even enemies, outcasts, and those who do not share the values and ideals of our own family or culture. There is no room for "tribalism" in a conscience transformed by faith in Jesus and the truth he reveals to us. While a faith-grounded conscience also remains rooted in the reasonableness of the golden rule, faith transforms that rule by transforming our understanding of who we are and who our neighbor is.

As catechists, we should be encouraged by this fact: Whatever we do to help children grow in faith and embrace Jesus' vision has a positive effect on their conscience formation. To put it another way, *all* catechesis is conscience formation even when we are not dealing with specifically moral issues. Also on the positive side is the fact that by thus nurturing the faith in any child, we are effectively challenging the distortions and half-truths to which all children are exposed as they grow.

To summarize: First, conscience formation of children has a natural, reasonable foundation, which is expressed by the golden rule and contained in the "law of God written in our hearts." Second, in a world wounded by sin, all children are exposed to cultural influences that can silence or distort their conscience. Finally, the conscience with its golden rule is transformed by faith, which offers us clear standards and reveals to us a radical new understanding of our own dignity and that of our neighbor.

THEOLOGY UPDATE

Morality and the Magisterium

For the Catholic Christian, the formation of conscience is never a solitary thing, never an isolated process. A Christian conscience cannot be formed in isolation from the wisdom of the past and the clear standards of the Christian community. In the simplest terms, a mature Christian conscience simply means to "put on the mind of Christ." But what is the "mind of Christ"? And how does one enter Christ's mind? The subject of conscience leads inevitably to the magisterium of the Church, the official interpreter of the "mind of Christ." Under the guidance of the Holy Spirit, the magisterium is responsible for protecting, preserving, and expressing all that God teaches through Scripture and the tradition of the Church. For the Catholic Christian who wants to put on the "mind of Christ," official Church teaching on faith and morals is the ultimate, objective standard for the formation of conscience.

In recent years, however, there has been a growing tension in the Catholic community. Reputable theologians have proffered certain approaches to contemporary moral issues that are at variance with traditional and clearly stated moral teachings of the Church. Though such teachings of the magisterium, like most, are not officially "infallible" declarations, they are teachings on faith and morals inspired by the Holy Spirit for the guidance of the faithful. Such teachings cannot be taken lightly.

Consequently, the magisterium has confronted some of these theologians with disciplinary action if they continue to promote contrary views. Theologians have countered that this interferes with the theologians' right of academic freedom within the Church and their duty to continue to probe the mysteries present in divine· revelation. How should we, as faithful Catholic Christians, view this debate, since it has far-reaching implications for the development of our own consciences? The following may help us form a responsible judgment.

First, it is important to clarify the special role the magisterium has in the life of the Church. Its primary responsibility is to protect, preserve, and express all that God teaches through Scripture and tradition. By its nature, the magisterium is a preserver. It has a duty to be conservative in its approach and to maintain a critical view of possible new interpretations of the Apostles' teaching as these are formulated. The magisterium is not conservative and cautious because of alleged personality quirks of high-placed officials in the offices of the Roman curia, but because of its very nature and mission as preserver. Also, we must keep in mind that the magisterium is responsible for official Church teaching *worldwide* and for the *entire future*. It feels no pressure to respond to "local" issues and accommodate its teachings piecemeal. It always must ask what impact a particular teaching or speculation will have on the *whole* Church. And it must ask what impact it may have on the foreseeable future. So the magisterium is never in a hurry to change (that is, reinterpret) an official teaching.

Finally, the magisterium has the responsibility to maintain the credibility of the Church's authentic and unerring interpretation of revelation as it affects our salvation. You will rarely find the magisterium officially and publicly announcing that the Church erred, even when the error does not reflect on the Church's ability to speak authoritatively on faith and morals. (One such example, however, occurred when the Church recently exonerated Galileo and admitted that its theologians mishandled that case in 1633.) Church doctrine evolves ever so slowly. It is the magisterium's duty to oversee that slow, orderly evolution, so that shifts and developments do not scandalize the faithful unnecessarily.

Having said this, we can see why confrontation between the magisterium and theologians is at times inevitable. Theologians are typically on the cutting edge. They use the official teachings of the Church as the "starting point" for new explorations into revelation.

They continually seek to find new ways to translate traditional teachings. They search for language and explanations that take into account new developments in society and human knowledge.

This kind of "confrontation" between the theologians and the magisterium can be found throughout Church history.

St. Thomas Aquinas, perhaps our most insightful theologian, introduced an innovation in theological explorations by drawing upon the writings of various pagan philosophers. His teachings were at first considered dangerous by the official Church, and for a time he was not allowed to teach publicly. In our time, Pierre Teilhard de Chardin was silenced by the magisterium, and his writings were suppressed. He has been exonerated posthumously. And even though many of his theological views are still not considered valid, neither are they regarded as a danger to the faith. So we need not be scandalized, on the one hand, if reputable theologians offer alternative views to traditional Church teachings on faith and morals. On the other hand, we need not be surprised or upset if the magisterium feels obligated to challenge and seek to restrain these theologians.

One other point that may help us understand the nature of the controversy between some of today's moral theologians and the magisterium is this: Traditional moral teaching of the Church has often been supported by arguments from the classical Aristotelian view of natural law. When arguments fail, however, and there seems to be no satisfactory reasons to bolster a difficult doctrinal position, the Church will simply take the flak and stand by its traditional faith and teaching in the matter. On the other hand, many of today's moral theologians, enriched by valid findings in the behavioral and physical sciences, find the classic natural-law approach inadequate. It once served us well, they would say, but now no longer. Many of these theologians operate out of a more phenomenological framework in their moral deliberations.

Just as the Church eventually adopted as its own the scholastic methodology perfected by St. Thomas, it is quite possible that the Church will in time adopt a more phenomenological approach to explain its moral teachings. But keep in mind, whatever system of philosophical or theological thought is used to support Church teachings, there always comes a time when all the categories are inadequate to explain matters of faith and doctrine. At that time the magisterium will stand by its traditional faith and teaching in the matter.

TEACHING TIPS

Where Your Treasure Is. . .

As a means to help your students get a better sense of their values, try this activity.

Invite the students to keep an exact account for one week of *every penny* they personally spend, regardless of how they received it — allowance, paper route, lunch money, etc. Provide each student with an expense sheet like the one below (or have them make their own in their notebook).

At the end of the week you have designated, they are to bring their "expense sheets" to class. Don't ask the students to share the details of the expense sheet, but do ask them to share anything they learned about their own values from this activity. Questions like the following can help in this sharing:

1. Were you surprised by anything on the expense sheet?

2. What percentage of your money did you spend on luxuries, or unnecessary items?

3. What percentage of your money did you spend on things that were intended primarily to make someone else happy?

Now discuss together Jesus' dictum "For where your treasure is, there also will your heart be" (Luke 12:34). Based on this expense sheet, where is their heart? End by challenging the students to identify one area where they will try to bring their values in closer alignment with those of Jesus.

Sample Expense Sheet

DAY/TIME	MONEY SPENT ON	AMOUNT	NEED/VALUE

See, Judge, Act

Here's a simple way to teach the students what is involved in making moral decisions. Resurrect the old but still valid Catholic Action formula "See, Judge, and Act."

Explain and discuss each component to ensure that the students understand them:

SEE: Be alert to what is really happening. Who is involved? Why? What circumstances are important? What motives are at work?

JUDGE: Does this situation promote or tear down the kingdom of God? Does it create peace and justice or strife and hurt? Does it promote and respect life, or does it disrespect and abuse life?

ACT: What should be *my* course of action in this situation? How and when am I going to act in this situation?

Present some sample situations to enable the students to practice this three-step process. For example:

1. How do you feel about copying someone's homework? Allowing someone to copy yours? What about copying on quizzes? Major tests?

2. Do you think you belong to a group or a clique? How does your class relate to and treat the children in the class below you?

Encourage them to use this simple formula any time they are not quite sure what they should be doing in a given situation. Even rather young children can follow this process.

Also invite the class as a group to use this process occasionally during the year to examine a problem or unique situation that arises in the school or neighborhood. For older children, it can also be the nuclear-arms issue and the drug problem.

The Act of Contrition

To help the students get beyond the words to the spirit behind the traditional Act of Contrition (or any other version you wish them to learn), try this. First, make sure everyone has memorized the words to the prayer formula you have chosen to use. You can do this through quizzes, class spelling-bee type recitations, etc.

Next, divide the class into small groups of three or four. Instruct each group to come up with a way to say the entire prayer using only gestures, facial expressions, and pantomime.

Have the groups take turns presenting their version of the prayer. It can be done in the form of a contest with the class picking the best version presented.

Variation: Do this as a class. Talk through the prayer, one phrase at a time. Ask for ideas of how it might be expressed in other words. Choose the best suggestion, make note of it, and go to the next phrase until you have alternate phrasing for the entire prayer. Practice together until you can say the whole Act of Contrition that way as a class.

You can use this approach with other prayers, too.

Signs for a Time

To help students develop a greater sensitivity to one another's feelings, try this activity.

First, explain to the class that *everyone* has the same basic need and desire to be treated with respect and concern. If we could simply remember this fact, we would probably treat one another as Christ taught us.

Next, provide each student with a strip of colored cardboard about three inches wide and eleven inches long, a piece of colored yarn, and a Magic Marker or crayons. The cardboard should have two holes punched in it large enough to pull the yarn through.

Instruct the students to make a sign on which they print the words I NEED TO FEEL IMPORTANT. If they wish, they can add other personal touches like a happy face and so forth. Then have them attach the yarn so they can hang the sign around their neck. The finished product should look something like the accompanying illustration.

Have the students write their name on the back of the signs, then collect them for the time being.

Now ask the students to develop and then discuss with you two lists that you write on the chalkboard. One list should contain ways they most dislike to be treated by others: things that make them feel embarrassed, angry, sad, or anything but important. The other list should contain ways others can treat them that will make them feel good about themselves. Behaviors in both lists should be as concrete as possible and realistic in terms of how this age-group in fact can and does treat one another.

In the process of developing these lists, help the students also identify some of the reasons we sometimes treat others badly and reasons why we sometimes fail to treat others with the respect and concern we know is right.

At the next class, as the students arrive, distribute the signs they had made previously. Instruct the students to put them on. Expect some initial embarrassment and giggles. Explain that they are to wear the signs simply as an experiment to see if they can help us remember how each of us wants and deserves to be treated.

Proceed with your regular class, but toward the end ask the students if seeing the signs in any way helped them to remember how to treat one another. Discuss as necessary. Collect the signs at the end of class.

Repeat this process for the next several classes. Then give the students this challenge as a homework assignment: They are to try to imagine that everyone they meet is wearing one of the signs they have been wearing in the class — children in other classes, other teachers, the bus driver, the crossing guard, people in the park or shopping mall, etc. They are to also try to treat them in the ways already discussed that can make people feel important and worthwhile.

At the beginning of the next class, ask the students to report on how well they were able to remember imagining that sign and what effects it had on their behavior. Invite them to discuss why it worked or didn't work for them.

Summarize by encouraging the students to continue this kind of experiment on their own, using it as an aid to remembering how Jesus wants us to treat one another.

Periodically when the class begins to show symptoms of being insensitive, resurrect the signs as a reinforcement.

Play God

Ask the students to imagine that they have the power to make everyone in the world follow three laws. Instruct them to write down the three laws they would want everyone to follow. (**Variation:** Instead of the world you can use the school, the class, or the city.) Ask the students to share their choices and explain the reasons for them. Then ask them to pick what they consider the best five laws presented — those they feel would make a perfect world (or school, class, etc.) if everyone followed them. Compare (or have them compare) their choices with the Ten Commandments, the beatitudes, or other key teachings of Jesus.

Signs of Love

Provide the students with a list entitled SIGNS OF LOVE. A sample list follows, but adapt it to your purposes:

I	II	III	
——	——	——	Saying "I'm sorry" and really meaning it.
——	——	——	Hugs and kisses.
——	——	——	Saying "I forgive you" and meaning it.
——	——	——	Helping someone without being asked.
——	——	——	Not complaining when being asked to help.
——	——	——	Doing a favor just to surprise someone.
——	——	——	Saying "Thank you" and meaning it.

Include as many "signs" as you wish. Instruct the students to complete the list as follows:

1. Check Column I if you saw someone do this during the past week.

2. Check Column II if you did this during the past week.

3. Check in column III the three that you think show the most love.

Ask the students to share the results of Columns I and III. Encourage them to give examples for Column I and reasons for Column III.

In the Other's Moccasins

As part of their moral development, the students need to begin to develop greater empathy toward the feelings of others. Role playing is a natural for this. For effective role playing with this age-group the following guidelines will help:

1. Encourage the role players to imagine as best they can how it would *feel* to be in the role-play situation. Be natural. Say and do what you *feel*.

2. Advise the "audience" not to worry about the "acting." Rather, they should be prepared to comment on how they might feel or what they might say or do in the same situation.

Do You Know How Good You Are?

Affirmation is an important part of moral development at any age. Try this with your class:

1. Prepare with your students a posterboard as follows:

There should be one square for every person in class including yourself. For example, fifteen students and one teacher means the board should have sixteen squares. Post the boards around the classroom.

2. Provide each student with a class list and with small squares of paper, one for every person in the class.

3. Instruct the students to decide one thing they really like about each person in class and write it on a square. They can also use symbols. The square is then pasted in one of the boxes on that person's board. Give examples such as "Good at math," "Great smile," "Always helping someone," and "You make us laugh." Stress that no put-downs will be tolerated. Have the students initial each square or leave the squares anonymous at *your* discretion.

4. After all the boards are completed allow each person to retrieve his or her board and review what it contains. This should be done in a reflective manner.

5. Close the activity by asking the students to give spontaneous expressions of thanks to God for one of the good things their friends see in them.

This can be a great community builder. It also forces the students to think more seriously about the good qualities their classmates do possess. Everyone wins!

Appropriate Game (Okay Game)

This is a classic that appears in a variety of forms. Here's one:

1. On a large poster board (or on the chalkboard) reproduce the following:

2. On separate index cards write a variety of actions related to moral or other topics you want the students to discuss. Here are some samples in the general area of moral behavior: smoking, reading sexually provocative magazines, eating junk food, drinking, jaywalking, passing off someone's else's work as your own, spending ten dollars on video games, sleeping with a teddy bear. (Adapt the actions to the issues you want to cover.)

3. Select a student to pick a card from the pile. He or she decides for whom such behavior is appropriate (morally acceptable) and places the card (makes an X) in the appropriate space. The student then explains to the group his or her reasons for the decision.

4. In turn, the remaining students state if they agree or disagree with the decision and explain their own reasons. You take a turn, too!

5. The first student (the one you selected initially) is then given a chance to change his or her original decision. He or she must explain the reason in either case.

6. Repeat the process with another student and continue as long as desired or until all have had a turn.

The Lost Commandments

Divide the class into small groups. Give each group a slip of paper with a commandment on it, *using the Fourth through the Tenth Commandments only*. The members of each group imagine that their particular commandment was not included in the original ten. They are to discuss and then list the possible consequences that would take place in their city (school, neighborhood) if no one ever followed that commandment. Circulate among the groups to stimulate their thinking. The groups should then share the results. The point is made quite well!

Family Project: Ten Commandments for a Happy Family

Have the students prepare two sheets of colored construction paper. On top of the first they print (artistically) TEN COMMANDMENTS FOR PARENTS. On the other, TEN COMMANDMENTS FOR CHILDREN. On each sheet they should write the numbers "1" through "10" on the left edge. Instruct them to ask their parents to fill out the second sheet (for children) while the students fill out the first (for parents). The students and parents should then share and discuss the results. Tell the students that the finished products should be posted in an appropriate place at home. After the project, ask the students to share with one another some of the "best" commandments from each list.

Projects

Junior high students love in-class projects. There is one rule of thumb, though. Give each person the opportunity to choose from a variety of possible ways to do a project. Let's say your theme is the sacrament of reconciliation and the Parable of the Prodigal Son. Each person is to do a project reflecting the core meaning of the parable. Some options might be a drawing, a poster, a bumper sticker, a collage, a mobile, a poem (perhaps a haiku), a personally composed prayer, a clay sculpture, a crossword puzzle, a thirty-second TV commercial, and a sock puppet "play." Since students' talents vary — some are verbal, some graphic, some imaginative, some manually skilled — you should allow the students the chance to choose the "medium" best suited to their talents. Also, don't hesitate to let two or three students work together if the situation allows. Peer sharing is critical for this age-group, especially in the area of moral education.

Chapter 12
Commandments and Beatitudes

The Ten Commandments (excluding the first three) can be arrived at by reason and defended by logic. In that sense, they are not too much different from the moral wisdom contained in pagan literature and the tribal codes of ancient times. Because they are logical and reasonable, there is a danger that we approach them that way in our catechesis. We are tempted to treat them individually, as isolated dictums, and emphasize the logic of obeying them, and the kinds of harm that result from disobeying them. This is not bad in itself, but it is limiting.

The commandments do not differ from the morality of pagan folk wisdom because they are original insights. They take on their unique quality as revealed moral truth because of the context in which they were promulgated, namely, within the overall Passover-Exodus-Covenant experience of the Hebrew people.

For the Hebrews, the commandments were an integral part of that saving, life-giving experience that set them apart as God's Chosen People. As such, the law itself was viewed as a life-giving, creative force. The Hebrews' very identity and continued existence as God's people and as a light to the Gentiles depended upon fidelity to these life-giving commandments. This is clearly evident in their history. Each time they strayed from fidelity to the law, they began to disintegrate as a people distinct from the pagans.

So the Ten Commandments and other elements of the law, though reasonable and logical, do not receive their unique moral force from logic or reason. Rather, they derive their moral force from the covenant with God and from faith in the God who saves. That's why the entire covenant law could be summarized by the law of love.

Jesus taught moral truth out of this same concept of covenant and faith in Yahweh, the God who saves. His moral teaching wasn't new in the sense that it contradicted the commandments and other moral precepts of the law. It was new and even radical because it was rooted in a perfected and therefore radical faith in the God who saves, his Father. As he himself said, he came to perfect the law, not to destroy it. That is, he came to renew and perfect the Jewish people's faith in God and in God's covenant love for them. Perfected faith results in a new, more radical appreciation of the commandments and what it means to *serve* God and neighbor. It results in a new, more radical understanding of what it means to *love* God and neighbor.

Jewish officials didn't oppose Jesus so much because they were scandalized by his teaching and feared he was corrupting the law; rather, their real fear was what would happen to the social order — and their positions of power and privilege within it — if the people actually began to live the law as perfectly as Jesus taught it. Radical faith in his Father's love gave Jesus' teaching freshness and authority, and the people marveled at it. It is only through that same faith that we can correctly perceive the life-giving force of his teaching in our lives. Jesus' Sermon on the Mount (Matthew 5 through 7) is best understood as the commandments and the law interpreted with such a perfected, radical faith.

For us catechists, then, the point to emphasize is this: The Ten Commandments and the moral teaching of Jesus should not be viewed or presented in the form of isolated moral truths. We need to perceive and present them within the overall context of our own covenant with the God who saves — where our *faith-filled* response to his saving action and his fidelity to us take place.

Granted, we need to treat specific moral truths, and we need to demonstrate the logic and reason behind them. But our catechesis should not be restricted to such a focus. Rather, our focus should be on faith in our own Passover-Exodus-Covenant as effected through Jesus' death and resurrection and through Pentecost. It is within that context that the commandments and the Christian moral code take on their true meaning. It is this context of faith that reveals their true meaning and their life-giving power. Love, not logic or fear, then becomes the motive for adopting them as our own.

THEOLOGY UPDATE

The Beatitudes

The beatitudes are often considered the epitome of Jesus' moral vision. They present a real challenge, however, not only as moral ideals but also in terms of interpreting what Jesus is revealing to us through them. Over the centuries, volumes have been written seeking to explain them. Debate among scholars continues. Here we will focus on only one approach, fully realizing other interpretations also give valid insights.

In our interpretation, the key lies in seeing them as a description of the ideal Jews of the Old Testament, those who achieved the radical faith in Yahweh and fidelity to the covenant, which Jesus sought to nurture. In the Old Testament, two types of people came closest to this ideal faith, and it is these two groups of people that Jesus describes in the beatitudes: the Anawim and the prophets.

The Anawim, or the poor in spirit, are those who fully recognize and accept their dependence on Yahweh, and fully trust in his providential love. The Anawim, in other words, are those who accept their status as contingent beings, dependent upon God for their very existence. This remains true regardless of their economic status or social position. This stance of authentic poverty, childlike trust, and total obedience wins for them special recognition as Yahweh's true children and the heirs to the kingdom of God.

From this acceptance of creaturehood flows authentic meekness, that is, the realization that true power is God's alone. Any power the Anawim do happen to possess is power put in total service to others. It is never used to coerce or oppress others. Such an exercise of power reflects authentic self-control and guarantees not only self-possession but ownership of the kingdom as well.

In the same way, the faith of the Anawim results in authentic mourning. Like the captive Anawim in Babylon, faithful Jews will always mourn whatever presently separates them from Yahweh and his kingdom. They won't waste tears on the inevitable loss of ephemeral goods or even life itself as much as they will grieve over separation from Yahweh.

Finally, the Anawim hunger and thirst not so much for earthly goods or physical satisfaction as for righteousness, for the perfection of their faith, and the perfection of their obedience to the covenant. In the first four beatitudes, then, Jesus reminds his Jewish audience of being Anawim — an ideal that could seem radical, even paradoxical, to those whose faith had been diluted by pagan concepts of blessedness and virtue.

In the second four beatitudes, Jesus recalls the ideals manifested by the prophets and reminds the Jews of their call to be like them — a prophetic people and a "light to the Gentiles." The foremost quality of prophets is to be merciful, to be proclaimers and witnesses to the creative, enduring mercy of Yahweh. The prophet may find it necessary to chide, to accuse, to remind people of their covenant responsibilities. But this is never done from a stance of haughtiness or self-righteousness. It is always tempered with the mercy of God and his re-creative power. Likewise, prophets are single-hearted (pure of heart) in their desire to proclaim faithfully and obediently only what God instructs them to proclaim. They aren't motivated by the desire for personal fame or personal gain. They are not distracted by needless speculation or by their own effectiveness to influence people. Prophets are peacemakers, promoting reconciliation and harmony rather than divisions and factions. They may evoke the wrath of others upon themselves, but they bring the peace of God to all who receive their message in faith.

That's why the sign of *persecution* will accompany one that is faithfully fulfilling the mission of prophet. Authentic prophets will inevitably evoke the wrath of the evil forces they expose and challenge. In that context, to be persecuted is in fact to be blessed (to be congratulated, as some exegetes translate the phrase) because it is positive assurance of God's approval of their ministry.

Obviously the message for us today is similar to the message presented to the Jews who gathered to hear Jesus at the Mount. We are called to have that radical faith of the Anawim — childlike, trusting, obedient to the covenant, and eager for its fulfillment. We are called to be prophets — single-hearted proclaimers and doers of peace and justice, courageous in persecution, and humble in success.

To the degree that we approach this kind of faith, we, too, will be blessed — and deserving of congratulations from Jesus.

TEACHING TIPS

Moses Mosaic

Divide the class into six groups and assign each group one of these aspects of Moses' life:
- Moses the Baby.
- The Young Prince.
- Called by God (Burning Bush).
- Leader of the Hebrew Exodus.
- Teacher of the Covenant.
- Leader in the Desert.

Give each group a piece of poster board. The groups are to *research* what the Bible says about their part of the Moses' story and decide how best to depict or symbolize it on their poster board. When they complete their work, the members of each group in turn present their poster and explain it to the class. Display the completed posters around the room or in the school corridor.

Let's Dream

Invite the students to imagine what kind of world would exist if everyone followed the Ten Commandments perfectly. Ask them to identify evils that would disappear if a particular commandment were followed by everyone. For example, we'd never have to lock our doors because no one would try to steal from us. The work of policemen would be entirely different. You may wish to use current newspapers. Ask the students to identify news stories that would be eliminated if everyone were keeping the commandments.

Finally, to make it more practical, turn the discussion to how life in their family, classroom, playground, and neighborhood would change if all of us tried to keep the commandments perfectly. List on the board specific benefits the students identify, then finish by challenging them to help create the kind of world they were *dreaming* about.

Prayer Pal

Try this every couple of weeks. Ask each student to write down one personal concern the student presently has — for example, a sick parent, a problem with school, alcohol, drugs. Collect all these *unsigned* petitions in a box or paper bag. Then pass the box around and ask each student to take out one slip.

In due time ask the students to share the results, if any, of a particular petition. Inevitably some will be able to report such good news, thus reinforcing in everyone the power and value of the prayer of petition.

Repeat the process of collecting and distributing new petitions.

Be careful, especially with younger students, to avoid giving the impression that this kind of prayer is *magic*.

Decisions, Decisions

To help the students become more conscious of the kinds of decisions they make, try this exercise. Have the students divide a sheet of paper into the following sections:
- From rising until going to school.
- From the beginning of school to lunch.
- During lunch hour.
- After lunch to the end of the school day.
- After school to supper.
- After supper to bedtime.

In each section, ask the students to write down any decisions they can recall making during that time slot yesterday. For example: decided to get up right away or decided to try to catch an extra ten minutes' sleep; decided to eat a good breakfast or to eat and run.

After you have helped the students recall at least one decision for each time slot, ask them to go back and try to associate any of the decisions with any of the Ten Commandments. For example: decided to eat good breakfast — Fifth Commandment; decided to do homework without being told — Fourth Commandment.

It's not necessary, nor is it usually possible, to associate every decision with a specific commandment.

Variation: Ask the students to mark decisions that ended up having good results with a plus (+) and those with negative results with a minus (-). Or ask them to identify decisions that had a good effect only for themselves with an *O* and those that had a good effect on more people than themselves with an *X*.

Using any of these kinds of approaches, lead the students to become conscious of the many decisions they are making each day and the potential their decisions have for making themselves and others happy — or sad.

What's a Good Excuse?

Begin by asking the students to think up crazy excuses for not having homework done. Some examples: "The dog ate it." "I was held captive in a spaceship all night and didn't escape in time to do the assignment."

Next, give the students some other situations like the following:

• Not paying attention at Mass.

• Not doing household chores until being asked several times and then doing them poorly.

• Avoid making an apology to someone you hurt in some way.

• Not forgiving someone who hurt you in some way.

• Wasting an evening watching junk on TV.

• Eating junk food.

• Littering on the way home from school.

Ask the students to give some typical excuses we might all use for acting in the ways described. In the process, review the difference between legitimate excuses and those we often use to *lie* to ourselves and/or others. Close by stressing how important it is that we don't get into the habit of *lying* to ourselves to avoid doing what we know we should do.

You Make the Rules

To help the students appreciate the role and importance of rules, divide the class into groups. Assign each group one of these kinds of jobs:

• School-bus driver.

• Zoo keeper.

• Movie-theater manager.

• Librarian.

• Teacher taking a group on a field trip to a museum.

• Baby-sitter taking a four-year-old to the store for a treat.

Have each group try to identify rules its members would feel necessary to make to ensure that they get their job done well. The groups must present and explain the rationale behind the rules they make.

Discuss this question together: Do people usually make rules to make people happy or unhappy?

Holy Name

Help the students search through the Old and New Testaments to find different names and titles used to describe God. Compile a list of these and together develop your own litany to the Holy Name of God. Use this occasionally as the opening or closing prayer of the class. Be sure to relate this activity to the Second Commandment.

Happiness Is. . .

Ask each student to write down on a slip of paper the one thing that could bring them the most happiness right now. It can be a material thing (such as a "boom box"), an event (such as winning the spelling championship or passing math), or an intangible thing (such as getting along better with parents or that Mom and Dad would make up). Instruct the students *not* to sign these.

After these are collected and shuffled, invite a student to pick one out and read it. Discuss the item in relation to the beatitudes and other Christian ideals related to true happiness. Repeat as often as time allows. Close by attempting to summarize the nature of true happiness as taught us by Jesus.

And the Winner Is. . .

Discuss with the students the various kinds of awards given each year to entertainers and sports figures, such as the Academy Award, the Emmy, the Tony, the Heisman Trophy, and the Cy Young Award (baseball pitcher).

Now ask the students to think up categories and names for awards that could be given to people who best uphold the ideals of the beatitudes and commandments — Peacemaker Award, Honesty Award, Pro-Life Award, Good Example Award, etc. After composing a suitable list of awards, discuss with the students which public figures — TV stars, rock stars, movie stars, sport stars, political leaders — deserve one or the other of these awards. Then reverse the question and discuss which ones least deserve such awards.

The activity can help the students view popular public figures more critically and with a more Christian perspective.

Chapter 13
Social Justice and Peace

Perhaps the most important task for the catechist wanting to teach social justice is nurturing an inner sense of solidarity, which is the link between awareness and action. Educating for justice and peace involves attitudinal change, not just content. The heart as well as the head must be educated. At least four elements are involved in this conversion process, which we need to consider for our own lives as well as for our students.

1. *Experiencing justice and peace as a call from Jesus.* The more that the call to justice and peace is seen as a call from Jesus, the more likely a person is to respond. Fostering a personal relationship with Jesus, especially through prayerful reflection on the prophets as well as the New Testament, is essential. Knowing that Yahweh and Jesus walk with us as we try to follow their call makes us more willing to say ''yes'' (see Jeremiah 1).

The liturgical year embodies the life of Jesus and hence his social mission. To make this mission explicit in the celebration of the liturgical year is essential in the conversion process. Advent and Christmas speak to us of the coming of Jesus in simplicity, to serve and not to be served. Lent marks the call to repentance for social sin as well as personal sin, the call to respond to Jesus as he suffers today, as his passion is relived in the hungry, the elderly, the victims of racism and repression.

The Eucharist itself calls us to build the unity of the Body of Christ, which we symbolize and celebrate at Mass. The music, the visuals, the kiss of peace, the prayers of the faithful can all remind us that the Jesus we hold up to God is the whole Body of Christ and that the ''yes'' we say to Jesus in Communion is a ''yes'' to the whole Body of Christ.

2. *Being touched by the advocates for justice.* People

working hard for justice, often at some risk, provide us with inspiration and imagination. The witness of people whose motivation is not financial gain and who find challenge and joy in working for change offers an important counter-model to the materialism all around us. The activities of these advocates for justice can also give all of us ideas about what we can do. We can invite them into our classrooms, even our homes, or we can go to where they are. Biographies are another way of providing such exposure, although less direct.

3. *Being touched by the victims of injustice.* For people who are not victims of injustice, such exposure has similar benefits, especially in terms of inspiration. Statistics about hungry people often do not touch our hearts and move us to action. There is an urgency about injustice that we do not experience generally unless we encounter the victims of that injustice, especially victims who are struggling against that injustice. Maryknoll films offer a less direct, though often powerful, experience. The handicrafts of economically poor people — through various outlets — enable us to meet the victims of injustice in their giftedness and to help them help themselves.

4. *Being supported in community.* Working for justice and peace often involves some risk. The support of others helps us overcome our fears, increases the effectiveness of our action, and provides both accountability and challenge. Also, working with others provides the necessary ingredient of enjoyment. Children especially need to enjoy social involvement if they are to integrate it into their own lives. Having other children along makes a real difference in many cases. Thus Christian service projects as part of the preparation for confirmation, for instance, might be designed to have students work in pairs or teams.

In conclusion, the more we lift up the lives and needs of others in prayer, the more we experience an inner sense of solidarity with them. And it is this growing inner sense of solidarity that makes us want to care and risk. Without it, neither we nor our students will ever move from awareness to sustained action.

Jim McGinnis
Institute for Peace and Justice

THEOLOGY UPDATE

The Church and Social Justice

Today, perhaps more than ever, the Church finds itself deeply involved in the public proclamation of social justice. We see not only Catholic laypersons in demonstrations for social justice but also priests, sisters, and bishops.

The issues cover a wide gamut of social problems confronting the

Christian of the twentieth century, such as equal rights for women and equal opportunities of employment for all. We hear the cries of battered women and minority groups such as blacks, Hispanics, gays, and farm workers. We read of the members of religious orders who stand up at stockholders' meetings of multinational corporations demanding changes in the unjust policies some of them have as standard operating procedure. We read with shock of the modern-day martyrs of Latin America who have lost their lives because they, as committed Christians, protested against social injustice.

Many of today's Catholics wonder what it's all about. Some write angry letters of protest to diocesan and national Catholic newspapers and magazines expressing the opinion that religious should stay in their churches, schools, or hospitals where "they belong."

What these people do not understand is that what is happening today has been happening since the human race became a part of life on this planet. The big difference now is that with instant communication we are being made more aware of it.

With a cursory look at the Old Testament one can find evidence of social injustice and the attacks of the prophets against it. These men, sent by God, sided with the "little people" — the oppressed and those who had no one else to stand up for them.

In the Gospel of Luke, when Jesus announced his mission he used the words of the Prophet Isaiah upon addressing the congregation in the local synagogue of Nazareth. He said: "The Spirit of the Lord is upon me, / because he has anointed me to bring glad tidings to the poor. / He has sent me to proclaim liberty to captives / and recovery of sight to the blind, / to let the oppressed go free, / and to proclaim a year acceptable to the Lord" (Luke 4:18-19).

And Jesus did just that. His closest companions, the people for whom he worked his miracles and almost all of those with whom he came in contact, were the suffering or the oppressed or the outcasts of their society. He attacked the oppression and the oppressors and demanded social justice. For this he gave his life.

In the fight for justice for all, as proclaimed by Jesus, the Church has had its good moments and its shameful ones as well. At times the Church has spoken out, but at other times it has been disgracefully silent in the face of social issues.

But the spirit of the prophets and the spirit of Jesus have once again come to center stage due to the documents of Vatican II, the encyclicals of recent popes, and the statements of many episcopal conferences throughout the world. Once more, Christians are beginning to realize that they are called to shout from the housetops for justice for all.

Walter Ong, S.J., wrote in *Theology Digest* that "Roman Catholic theology has the advantage of its own long history. It has been on the scene a long time. It is the direct heir, not the indirect or the adopted heir, but the direct heir, of two thousand years of continuous reflection since the advent of the Word as man. We have theological riches that no other group can claim and we should honestly avow this fact and not dodge the responsibility it entails.''

That responsibility is to use the teachings of Jesus Christ in the struggle to make the world better by creating a world in which injustice does not exist. And each of us is called into this struggle and pledged to it by reason of our baptism and confirmation. Where injustice exists, the Christian cannot sit by idly and silently. We are called just as Jesus was called.

Cardinal Count Galen, on July 13, 1941, speaking out against the atrocities being committed against the Jews of Germany said: ''. . . (Justice is the state's foundation.) We lament, we regard with great concern, the evidence of how this foundation is being shaken today, how justice — that natural and Christian virtue, which is indispensable to the orderly existence of every human society — is not being plainly implemented and maintained for all. It is not only for that of the rights of the human personality, it is also out of love for our nation and out of our profound concern for our country that we beg, ask, demand: Justice!'' (See *The Nazi Years: A Documentary History*, published by Prentice-Hall.)

We, the Christians of the United States, must demand the same wherever and whenever we find an act of injustice, be it in government policy toward Latin America or in the social programs or lack of them in our cities and towns.

The fight against social injustice is nothing new. It is as old as the human race because there has always been present among us those who would deny others their human rights and dignity.

We, as Christians, have been called to be the salt of the earth (Matthew 5:13) and the leaven in the dough (Matthew 13:33). We have been called ''to bring glad tidings to the poor'' and ''to let the oppressed go free'' (Luke 4:19).

We — laity, priests, sisters, and bishops — cannot permit the evil of social injustice to exist. If we do, we will also be judged guilty of injustice for our failure to respond to our call and our anointing.

Father Gerry Bouressa
Diocesan Priest/Missionary to the Dominican Republic

TEACHING TIPS

Be Creative

Ask the students to identify some typical conflict situations they experience at home, at school, at play. For example: arguments over whose turn it is to do dishes, what TV program to watch, who gets first turn, who decides what game to play.

In small groups, have the students seek to come up with three or four alternatives to resolve such conflicts in ways that would be fair for all involved. They then share these with the other groups to decide the best ways to resolve the conflicts and restore peace.

Use this same technique when conflict situations arise within the class or within the school. The experience helps the students begin to realize that a little creativity can resolve most day-to-day conflicts they encounter in ways that allow everyone to win.

Family Project

Ask the students to discuss with their parents and other family members ways in which to conserve and make better use of the gifts they have. For example: Turning off lights, taking a shorter shower, eating everything on one's plate, walking rather than using the car all the time. They may also want to identify something special to do like having a meatless day once a week or skipping desserts once a week.

Such a list can be posted at home. Each time a person does one of these things he or she initials that item on the list. One of the parents can keep track of the money saved by these conserving activities. This money, saved by all members of the family, can then be given to the Society of St. Vincent de Paul or a similar group that cares for the poor.

Gift Giving

Gifts need not be bought. Children can make all kinds of delightful presents for special occasions. Besides the ones made from crafts, gifts of time and love mean so much. To give coupons of service to a loved one makes the gift special for quite a while. These coupons of tasks done, of little extras that make family life a happy time, can be redeemed at the discretion of either the giver or the receiver. A book of coupons, such as the accompanying example, can be decorated to suit the occasion.

Mercy

Have the students memorize the corporal and spiritual works of mercy. Assign one work to each student or pair of students. Each makes a poster upon which the work is printed artistically. It can then be decorated with an appropriate drawing or a picture from old magazines. Leave some blank space on each poster.

Hang the posters around the room. Each time a student does one of these works he or she can initial that poster in the blank space. Challenge the students to try to initial as many of the posters as they can within a certain time limit.

Cooperate

Challenge the children in small groups to try to develop games that require cooperation by participants rather than competition. An example is Balloon Pass. The group stands in a circle. Each person keeps one hand behind the back. A balloon is presented to the group. The object is to pass the balloon around and across the group by tapping it with the free hand. Count hits out loud. After the balloon hits the floor, the group begins again, trying to get more hits the next time.

As a group develops a cooperation game let its members demonstrate the game before the whole class.

Follow the games by some discussion about the value of cooperation as opposed to competition in play activities. How does it feel when everyone wins rather than dividing persons into groups of winners and losers?

Slogans/Bumper Stickers

Challenge your students to make peace-and-justice bumper-sticker slogans (for instance, "If you want peace, work for justice"). If you want to take it a step farther, provide contact paper so that the students can make stickers to put on the family car. The process of making up slogans helps the students clarify the issues.

TV Or Not TV

Have the students list their five favorite TV programs. Instruct them to rate each one on a scale of 1 to 5, "5" being excellent, using the following criteria:

✓ Does it promote concern for others?

✓ Does it present women in a wholesome, well-balanced manner, as opposed to being presented as "sex objects," for example? How about men?

✓ Does it treat violence as an evil?

✓ Does it promote understanding between races and between sexes?

Ask the students to share the results of their work. Then discuss the value of each program in terms of Gospel values. Finally, ask the students to decide if their programs deserve to be watched. Why or why not?

The above criteria are simply examples. Make up your own if you wish to focus on a particular value related to justice and peace. This can serve as a lead-in to the overall topic of how our society's values often contradict Gospel values.

Male and Female

Ask the students to list as many words as they can think of that contain the word "man" or that end in "man." For example: mailman, chairman, mankind. Then ask the students to try to come up with alternative words that are not sexist. For example: mail carrier, chairperson, humanity.

Follow with a discussion of some of the kinds of sexism they can still encounter in today's society, and the injustices involved.

Remind them to try to avoid sexist words in class or in any writing they do for you.

Let Us Pray

An effective prayer service can be created from the newspaper. Ask the students to bring to class an article depicting an injustice. If the article is long, just use the headlines. The service consists of a reading from one of the prophets, the Our Father, and an extended prayer of petitions using the newspaper reports. To each account of injustice, all respond: "Lord, give us your healing and let all people be free."

The Need for Social Justice Is Nothing New

Divide the students into small groups and assign one chapter from one of the prophets and have them find the social evil and the prophet's response against it. These can be shared with the entire class. The prophets best used are Jeremiah, Hosea, Amos, and Jonah.

Stereotypes

Write on the board Jew, Indian, Italian, Mexican, Polish, Black, Oriental, etc. Have the students jot down the first five things that come to mind regarding each ethnic group. Review their thoughts with them, determining which ones have been given us through the media or books as stereotypes and are prejudicial. Which characteristics are common to all people? Which ones are unique to a particular people? Which ones need to be erased?

If you happen to have minority members in your class, you might ask them to share some of their own experiences of prejudice and stereotyping. Obviously this would have to be handled with sensitivity.

Discuss the injustice of prejudice and stereotyping.

People Doing Justice

Your students should know how justice is being achieved in their community. At least one session each year can be spent on a community awareness session. Invite all agencies, societies, and associations in the community that are involved in service or eliminating an injustice to share their work with the students and their parents. The sharing can be done either with a display area or by brief talks outlining their respective programs. If there are too many agencies to invite, limit them to those in which you want the students to participate. Examples: St. Vincent de Paul Society, Bread for the World, Meals on Wheels, volunteer groups, and political action groups.

As an alternative you can conduct field trips to various community service agencies.

More People Doing Justice

Provide the students with lists of the beatitudes and the corporal and spiritual works of mercy. Using newspapers over a week's time, the students are to find at least one example of each work and beatitude being practiced. Part of the project might be to put together a "scrapbook" in which they paste the articles on appropriately labeled pages.

After the students share their work, have them discuss some of the kinds of practices that are well within their reach.

Helping Hands

This perennial activity is always effective in relation to the topic of compassion. You will need a fairly large box, covered with butcher paper. Divide the class into five groups and assign each group responsibility for decorating one side of the box with pictures of "helping hands." Using old magazines, newspapers, etc., each group must find pictures of "helping hands" to cut out and paste on their side of the box. Also, each group member should trace his or her hands on the box and sign it. Discuss each side in turn, making a special effort to solicit practical ideas of some of the helping activities that the students can carry out. Also, seek to identify hurting people within their immediate community to whom they could reach out.

Helping Career Days

Periodically, perhaps once a month, invite a different person from the community who is engaged in a helping career or in a helping volunteer work to address the class. Some possibilities to consider might be a physical therapist, military-draft counselor, a St. Vincent de Paul or Good Will worker, a translator for the deaf, a legal-aid lawyer, a free-clinic worker, a home nurse, or a Meal-on-Wheels volunteer. The guest should be asked to share information regarding the particular needs or problems of his or her clients within the community and also share ideas about how the students can themselves get involved. Share all that is involved in preparation for the particular career.

Helping Career Study Centers

As a variation of the above, form the class into groups. Assign each group to do research on a particular helping career or volunteer agency that seeks to help or overcome a particular need within the community. Each group is to prepare a study center. The center should include posters, pictures, pamphlets, charts of statistics, etc., related to the problem and the helping career. This is also important: Each group should prepare a *handout* with four or five practical suggestions of what students their age can do in relation to the problem or need. (You may have to help them get these handouts duplicated, one for each student in the class.)

On a given day, the groups can set up their study center in various areas of the classroom. You may want to provide each group with a card table. While one member of the study group takes his or her turn at the groups' study center, others are free to visit each of the other centers.

Variation: You may consider setting up these booths in the school cafeteria for other classes to visit during lunchtime or they can be set up in conjunction with a home/school meeting.

This approach is a very effective means for other topics, including various religions, various periods in Church history, the various religious vocations (married, single, religious, priest), even the different sacraments. The key is in the kind of research the group must do and the kinds of handouts the group is asked to prepare.

Compassion Bulletin Board

Suitably decorate or ask the students to decorate a section of your bulletin board as a COMPASSION CORNER. Invite the students to bring in newspaper and magazine articles dealing with examples of people showing compassion to others. They can also be asked to bring in stories related to people who are hurting and in need of help. Discuss the material periodically and/or use it as themes for class prayer.

Call-In Game

This variation on role playing can be used for dealing with a wide variety of religious, moral, and emotional concerns — for example, peer pressure, parental authority, cheating on tests, boredom at Mass, shyness, and going to confession. With your students, identify and briefly describe on a 3'' x 5'' card the situations you want to treat. Keep the description general (for instance, your friend keeps wanting to copy from you during tests). Select a panel of about four students. Appoint one as host — or you may prefer to play this role. Pass out the first situation card to a volunteer student. Have the student "call" the radio show and state his or her problem. Encourage the caller to role play, embellishing and trying to make the call as realistic as possible. To add to the realism, use a toy phone for the callers and a toy microphone (or make-believe mike) for the panel. The panel should respond to the call with advice. The caller may ask other questions or comment in response.

After the "call," ask the whole class to react to the panel's advice. Did everyone in the class agree with it? What would the students have added, not said, etc.? Add your own comments as necessary. After processing the first call in this way, change panels, select a new caller, and repeat the process. This game can be used as a "filler" activity or can be played on a regular basis — for example, every other Friday. Once the students get into the spirit, this role-play variation is an excellent means of both finding out how students are thinking and for treating some tough issues in a nonpreachy way.

In dealing with a question, first solicit ideas from the students — for instance, "Why do you think God allows innocent people to suffer?" Reinforce valid insights, correct erroneous ones, and then share your own insights, based on the study you have been able to do concerning the question. In the proper context you can help the students develop a better understanding of the concept of faith in relation to mystery.

Ten Commandments for Peace in the Classroom

Ask the students to identify typical conflict situations they encounter among themselves within the class and on the playground.

List these and then ask the students to identify the most common causes behind these conflict situations. Examples could include selfishness, impatience, thoughtlessness, and misunderstanding.

Have the students, working in small groups, develop a list with the heading TEN COMMANDMENTS FOR PEACE IN THE CLASSROOM, aimed at countering the causes for conflict. Encourage the groups to make these as practical as possible.

After the groups share the results, have the class decide on the best ten ideas that emerge. Print or have your most artistic student print these on poster board, decorating it appropriately and displaying it in the classroom.

Current Events

Make a current events bulletin board. Divide the board down the middle and give it two headings: WAR and PEACE. Encourage the students to bring in articles and pictures from the daily newspaper that reflect the violence, hatred, division, and injustice we find in the world. Also, they are to look for material dealing with peacemaking efforts, reconciliation, cooperation, and the correcting of injustices. Articles can deal with local, national, and international events. A particular day each week can be assigned for bringing in the material. Ask the students to present their findings to the class and discuss them as time allows. Select or have the students select the material to be placed on the board for the next week. As an option, collect all the material and change the board every day during the next week. This can be a very good, ongoing activity to help sensitize students to the violence in society as well as to alert them to all the good work that is going on to promote a peaceful and just society.

Peacemaker

Begin by asking the class to complete this sentence: Peace is. . . Use the students' responses for a discussion on the meaning or definition of peace, then attempt to arrive at a class definition of peace (what it means for that age-group, in contrast to some philosophical, abstract definition).

Next, have the class come up with five words that describe a peacemaker. From all the words given, have the members of the class choose the five they think are the best. Now direct the students to read the following or similar Gospel passages that present Jesus' reactions to conflict situations:

- Luke 7:11-17, 10:25-37, 18:15-25.
- John 9:1-12.
- Matthew 5:21-26, 5:43-48, 8:1-13, 15:29-31.

Discuss Jesus' words and behavior. Have the students compare his approach to peace and peacemaking with their own ideas.

Survey the Situation

Help the students develop a simple questionnaire on peace that they can give to their parents and one or two other adults. Sample questions would touch on some of the following:

1. Are you familiar with the peace pastoral written by the United States bishops?

2. Are you in favor of banning nuclear weapons?

3. Are you ever afraid there really might be a nuclear war?

4. Do you think people opposed to nuclear weapons are unpatriotic?

5. What do you think is the best way to make the world peaceful and to avoid future wars?

Have the students report back their results to the class. Discuss the different opinions that surface.

This activity does several things. It can get parents involved in thinking about the issues raised and talking about them with their children. It can help students see that there are many different opinions and no easy answers to the problems of war and peace. Finally, it can serve as a jumping-off point for motivating the students to identify and undertake a class project to promote more peace awareness within the parish or local area. Sample projects might be:

1. Raise money to buy space in the parish bulletin or local newspaper for a peace message developed by the students.

2. Make posters or sponsor a poster contest for the whole school; arrange with local merchants to display the posters in their store windows or similar public places.

3. Adopt a child or family in one of the war-torn areas of the Middle East or Latin America; the students can write to the person (or persons) and hold fund-raising projects to send aid.

4. Have a letter-writing project in which the students make their thoughts known to the editor of the local newspaper; or they can send letters to the president and their senator or representative in Washington.

Keep in mind that such activities should be as tangible as possible. However, the real effect is to help develop a sense of personal responsibility for promoting peace in the world. These activities can have long-range results as the students reach adulthood.

Plan a Peace Day or a Peace Week

Involve the students in planning a peace day or peace week for the entire school. It can include such activities as a school-wide prayer service or liturgy, a film, a poster contest for each grade level, a guest speaker like a visiting missionary, and a reconciliation service. Encourage the students to think in terms of involving their parents in the activities as much as possible.

Chapter 14
Catechesis for Children with Disabilities

CATECHETICAL REFLECTION

A quiet revolution has been taking place in our society for the past thirty years. It has been initiated and led by many unnamed heroes of great compassion and vision. Their efforts are beginning to reshape the thinking and the very physical surroundings of much of the Western world. In short, they are radically altering our society's awareness, understanding, and treatment of our handicapped citizens.

The visible effects of this revolution are appearing everywhere. They don't seem that dramatic — unless, of course, you or a loved one has a handicap. All the newer public buildings and recently remodeled ones, for example, now include access ramps, wider doors, and direction signs for the sight impaired. There are drinking fountains and toilet facilities that can accommodate people in wheelchairs. Curb ramps are appearing at our street corners, as are sound signals at traffic lights. Speakers at public gatherings are simultaneously signed for the hearing impaired. Closed-captioned TV is available, as is special telephone equipment. Public transportation is being adapted and made available to the handicapped. These physical changes reflect one level of this revolution.

Advocates have been promoting the constitutional right of all citizens to have reasonable access to the basic necessities and amenities we take for granted. Laws ensuring this right are now on the books and are quietly being implemented.

But there is a second and more profound level to this revolution. The advocates for the handicapped are gradually altering thousands of years of prejudice and stereotyped attitudes. These erroneous attitudes run the gamut from total avoidance to condescending paternalism to sick humor and the "freak show" mentality.

The revolution at this level reflects a fundamental Gospel truth:

every human being has dignity and worth. In a materialistic world view, dignity and worth are "earned" in proportion to accomplishments in productivity and usefulness. In the Gospel vision, Jesus teaches us to value love and humility, hope and faith, patience and compassion. The "handicapped" are those blinded by greed or ambition, crippled by pride or hatred, deafened to the cries of the widow, the orphan, and the helpless.

Such a vision, proclaimed by the advocates of the handicapped, is truly revolutionary. It turns our current world and its values upside down.

As catechists we are called to support and continue to promote this revolution at both levels. We are called to sensitize ourselves and our students to the physical needs of the handicapped and to promote their right to be integrated into the mainstream of society's life.

More importantly, we are called to promote and protect the *dignity* of the handicapped as valued and valuable citizens in the kingdom of God and in our society. They don't want pity. Like all human beings they seek respect and the opportunity to earn that respect. They don't whine for special treatment. They simply ask for the basic support and encouragement we all seek.

The rights and dignity of the mentally handicapped present us with a special challenge. In many instances, those with physical disabilities are still capable of great achievements according to the standards of a materialistic society. We all know stories of blind musicians, deaf inventors, computer geniuses, or successful business executives confined to wheelchairs. These stories tend to make us more tolerant of the physically handicapped. There is *hope* for them. They may still "contribute." But what about the mentally handicapped?

As catechists, we have a special challenge. We must strive to sensitize ourselves and our students to the rights, dignity, and unique value of the mentally handicapped in our society. In the THEOLOGY UPDATE section, which follows, we'll expand on this important topic as it confronts the Church.

THEOLOGY UPDATE

The Mentally Handicapped

(Note: the expressions "mentally handicapped" and "mentally disabled" are generally considered synonymous today and both are acceptable.)

The Church, in imitation of Jesus, has always been in the vanguard of society in promoting the rights and dignity of the handicapped. However, the Church's relation to the mentally handicapped has presented a particular challenge. Their limited capacity for abstract thought seemed to exclude the possibility, and the necessity, for any kind of formal catechesis. By extension it seemed to exclude them from the sacramental life of the Church with the exception of baptism. This was eventually supported by certain theological principles. Since the Lateran Council of 1215 "the age of reason or discretion" became a necessary criterion for readiness to receive the Eucharist. Since some of the mentally handicapped are incapable of achieving that stage of development, it seemed to preclude the possibility for them to be able to join the community at the Eucharistic table. For the same reason there was no obligation to attend Mass. In that same period the presence of sin after baptism was determined as a necessary criterion for a valid celebration of the sacrament of reconciliation. The mentally handicapped were judged incapable of sin in any formal sense. So they were likewise excluded from the sacrament of reconciliation. Catechesis to prepare the mentally handicapped was judged unnecessary as a result. By extension formal catechesis of any kind was considered impossible. It was often reduced to teaching the most rudimentary prayers and gestures like the Sign of the Cross, if any attempt was made at all.

Since formal catechesis was neither necessary or possible in the popular sense, the Church felt no responsibility to offer it. Any effort at all in this area was left solely to the discretion of the parents or guardians of the mentally handicapped persons.

For many reasons too involved to explain here, this attitude of excluding the mentally handicapped from the sacraments and from formal catechesis has radically changed in recent years. Most simply, many contemporary movements have radically altered our understanding of the nature of the mentally handicapped's capacities, needs, and rights as baptized members of the Church.

As a result the Church now sees that formal catechesis for the mentally handicapped is both possible and desirable. More significant, participation in the sacramental life of the Church is also seen as both possible and desirable.

These convictions have resulted in some tangible benefits, not just for the mentally handicapped persons and their families, but for the Church as a whole. For example, the desire to make the Eucharist available to the mentally handicapped has helped us to rediscover and reclaim a part of our tradition and theology of the Eucharist that had been lost to us over the centuries. In the early Church, a fundamental understanding of the Eucharist centered on the concept of belonging. Baptism united us to Christ and the community. The Eucharist celebrates and nurtures that union. It seemed logical to the early Church, therefore, that infants and small children already united to Christ and the Church by baptism should join the community at the Eucharistic table much like they join the family at the ordinary meals.

This was such a widespread practice and conviction that the English archbishop of Canterbury, Lanfranc, wrote a strong letter to his Irish clergy in 1089 complaining that some of the priests were denying little babies Communion. He reminded them that the practice of excluding them was not permitted, neither here nor across the sea.

A theology of the Eucharist that emphasizes the concept of belonging provides the contemporary justification for preparing and bringing the mentally handicapped to the Eucharistic table. Even if the person never reaches the capacity to reason ordinarily required, he or she can both grasp the meaning and experience the desire to belong to the community of believers, including the Eucharistic community.

At the same time, by reclaiming this theological aspect of the Eucharist, the Church at large has been helped to move from a too self-centered and formalistic theology of the Eucharist that evolved after the Lateran Council.

In much the same way reconciliation is best understood as "coming home" to the Eucharistic community by removing the sin that has alienated us from it. Even if the mentally handicapped can't sin or understand sin in the formal sense, they are capable of experiencing alienation and of committing material acts that do alienate them. They can experience the desire to be reunited and to be forgiven by the community to which they belong. This theology of reconciliation goes to the heart of the sacrament and is sufficient to allow at least the less severely handicapped, even given their verbal limitations, to have access to the joy of forgiveness and reunion the sacrament is intended to offer us. Reemphasizing this aspect of reconciliation has helped the whole Church shift its focus away from preoccupation with the fear and shame associated with confessing our sins and toward the joy, peace, and reunion Jesus is offering us in the *celebration* of forgiveness of our sins.

Finally, as the Church's commitment to formal catechesis for the mentally handicapped has grown we have been forced to review all the basic truths of our faith with "new eyes." We have been forced to seek ways to express highly technical and abstract theological formulas in language and images a small child can grasp. This search for simplicity has actually made many of these truths more accessible and understandable to all of us. It has also pioneered new, creative, highly imaginative and experimental methods of catechesis that are effective for all age levels, not just the mentally handicapped.

In short, in our very efforts to respond to the needs of these "little ones" in our midst it is we ourselves who have probably benefited the most. The mentally handicapped are enriching the life of the whole Church in much the same way they enrich the lives of the families and individuals who embrace them and take them into their hearts. They enrich us not just by the love, warmth, affection, innocence, trust, and generosity that is innately theirs but also by the challenge they give us to grow in our own understanding and appreciation for the gift of faith that is ours. "Love grows by giving it away."

TEACHING TIPS

Wrong Handed

A nonthreatening way to sensitize students to at least some of the plight and frustrations experienced by the physically handicapped is the following:

1. The next time you plan to work on a class project like making posters, form your groups in the usual way. However, identify certain members of each group as "handicapped." They must participate and follow all the directions for the activity. But they must keep their "good hand" behind their back. (For these age-groups we don't recommend the practice of tying the hand behind the back as is sometimes done. It can actually distract from the purpose of exercise.)

2. At the end of the activity review the experience by asking these questions:

For the nonhandicapped: What was your attitude toward the "handicapped" in your group? Did you find yourself getting impatient with them? Were you tempted to laugh or tease, or did you find yourself wanting to help? Did you note that the "handicapped" members have the same needs as you — success, respect, belonging, contributing to the group?

For the "handicapped": What were some of your strongest feelings? Anger? Embarrassment? Frustration? Did you feel that the others accepted you as an equal or did they treat you differently? How would you like them to treat you?

Use the exercise and the student responses as a lead-in for presenting ideas regarding the rights and dignity of the handicapped and the Christian attitude toward them.

Crime of Innocence

If possible, show and discuss the film *Crime of Innocence*, produced by Paulist Productions. It very effectively deals with the stereotypes and prejudices toward the mentally handicapped that are still too prevalent in our society. It can serve as a good starting point for discussing the proper Christian relationship to the mentally disabled.

Check the Premises

Divide the class into teams. The teams are to survey the parish premises: school, church, rectory, etc. They are to list all instances where the physically handicapped are being denied reasonable access. Access means to parts of the building themselves (for example, second floor) or to necessities and amenities: toilets, drinking fountain, pop machine, etc.

They should also list those adaptations to the environment that have been made in consideration of the handicapped — especially marked parking places, ramps, etc.

As a variation you can assign each team a particular handicap: confined to a wheelchair; confined to crutches; blindness; deafness. Have each team survey the premises with their particular handicap in mind, then have the teams report their findings.

Older students could also be asked to research the costs involved in making suggested changes in the environment. They could then be challenged to undertake a project to raise the funds and promote one of the changes.

Be sure to go through proper channels before you undertake such a project.

Witness

You should be able to find various people within the parish community who could give an effective "witness" in behalf of the physically or mentally handicapped. If done sensitively, a student who is personally handicapped or who has a handicapped member in the family can be invited to "tell the story."

You could also invite parents of a mentally handicapped child or adults who are physically handicapped to share their experiences with the class. Such firsthand sharing can have a powerful influence on developing the sensitivity of the students.

Vocabulary Check

Have the students identify those words used as put-downs in everyday conversation that have their roots in some form of mental or physical handicap — for example, spastic, retard, moron. List these words on the board.

Discuss the implication of using such words as putdowns. What attitudes do they reflect concerning the dignity of the handicapped?

Encourage the students to remove such words from their active vocabulary. Invite them to remind one another of the offensiveness of such words whenever they're used.

Jesus Led the Way

Jesus' example is the foundation of the Church's commitment to the physically and mentally handicapped. A good way to illustrate this is as follows:

1. Form the class into teams and provide each team with a copy of the New Testament.

2. Identify a particular Gospel or several specific chapters in a Gospel.

3. Instruct the teams to find within a set time limit as many occasions as they can in which Jesus showed compassion for the handicapped. Explain that lepers and those possessed by devils would also have been classified as handicapped by the people of his time.

4. Have the teams share the results. The team that identifies the most occasions wins.

Follow with a discussion of Jesus' attitude toward the handicapped. Ask the students to identify key words or phrases that might summarize or symbolize that attitude. Some examples might include involved, approachable, and defender.

Summarize by emphasizing that as followers of Jesus we are called to make those attitudes our own.

Not Quite a Telethon

Invite the students to develop a school or parish-wide campaign to help promote the rights and dignity of the handicapped. Some elements of the campaign could be the following:

1. Have the class develop a slogan and symbol for the campaign.

2. Have the class make and sell buttons (or give away buttons) on which the slogan or symbol is depicted.

3. Have the class make posters to distribute around the school.

4. Have the class sponsor a poster contest among all grades. The winning posters (three places) at each grade level will then be displayed in some prominent place in school. Other posters will be returned for display in individual classrooms.

Have the class sponsor an "essay" contest for the middle and upper grades. Contestants must complete the following statement in fifty words or less: "Concerning the handicapped a Christian will always. . ." The class then reads and picks winners for each grade level represented. The winning essays will then be duplicated and circulated in a special bulletin sent to all the classes, the school paper, or in a newsletter.

The class could approach the Home-School organization to provide some token prizes for the various contests. The overall campaign could be tied to a fund-raising project to make some environmental change on the parish premises that would make them accessible to the handicapped.

Learn 'Signing'!

Teach or invite someone to teach the students to sign the alphabet. They will enjoy learning it, and it is relatively easy to learn. It can be useful to them on occasions, enabling them to establish a basic communication with the deaf.

As a variation, teach the students or invite someone to teach them how to sign certain greetings and expressions that can be used in relating to the deaf — for example, "I love you." (*Signs for Catholic Liturgy and Education* can be purchased from the National Catholic Office for the Deaf, 814 Thayer Ave., Silver Spring, MD 20910. The price is $5.00 plus postage and handling.)

Teach them to sign the Lord's Prayer and some of the parts of the Mass, like the greetings, the Holy, Holy, and the Lamb of God.

A fun drill in teaching the students to sign the alphabet is to have a spelling bee in signing. You say the word and they must sign it back to you. Or you sign the word and the student says it. Conduct it like a regular spelling bee or form teams.

Write a Collect

Provide the students with samples of the Collect prayers selected from some of the major feasts. Use them as good examples of prayers that capture in a few words the nature and purpose of the feast.

Invite the students, working alone or in teams, to compose a Collect that might be used for a liturgy that focuses on the rights and dignity of the handicapped as well as on their difficulties and needs.

Use these over a period of time to open or close your classes. The task of writing them is a good exercise to help the students clarify their ideas and attitudes about the handicapped. The use of the prayers serves as a good reinforcement and periodic reminder of proper attitudes.

Resources

BOOKS

An excellent resource related to the handicapped is *A Teacher's Handbook for Children with Disabilities*. This supplement to the *I Am Special — Level 2* program offers practical advice on how to use *I Am Special* for special-education classes. The book includes hand signs for the hearing impaired, teaching techniques for a variety of handicapped children, ages four to fourteen, recommended activities, exercises, and music. It is available from Our Sunday Visitor, 200 Noll Plaza, Huntington, IN 46750. Call toll-free 1-800-348-2440.

* * *

A ten-page manual identifying the causes and manifestations of child abuse is available from the Board of Parish Services, Lutheran Church-Missouri Synod, 1333 S. Kirkwood Road, St. Louis, MO 63122. It provides detailed suggestions for steps a teacher should take when abuse is suspected, as well as telltale signs for detecting the problem. Since this problem touches all economic, educational, and ethnic groups, we can't presume "it's not happening to our students." The title of the manual is *Child Abuse: What Can Teachers Do About It?*

* * *

A book that will speak to some women in today's Church is aptly entitled *Beyond Anger: On Being a Feminist in the Church*, by Carolyn Osiek (Paulist Press, $4.95). She argues for the value of suffering and the need to remain within the Church in order to maintain the struggle for women's rights.

* * *

Paulist Press, in cooperation with the National Conference of Religious Vocation Directors, has put together a new edition of *Ministries for the Lord*. It can serve as an excellent resource if you happen to be studying religious communities. It presents the history and related background on each community treated, plus current information on their work, statistics, etc. Cost: $4.95. Write: Paulist Press, 997 MacArthur Blvd., Mahway, NJ 07430. Telephone: (201) 825-7300.

Of related interest, the National Sisters Vocation Conference has published a slide production entitled *Women Religious: Called to Life and Service*. It depicts women religious involved in all aspects of their ministry, prayer, and community life. Purchase for $40.00; rent for $15.00. Write: NSVC, 1307 Wabash, Suite 350, Chicago, IL 60605.

* * *

Have trouble pronouncing Eutychus? Or any other names of people and places in the Bible? Check out the *Lector's Guide to Biblical Pronunciations*, which gives you phonetic spelling of all the hard-to-say names and places in the Bible. Developed by Joseph M. Staudacher. Our Sunday Visitor Publications, $2.62.

* * *

Looking for bilingual materials for Hispanic catechesis? Our Sunday Visitor has recently added two Spanish/English products to its very popular *I Am Special* (IAS) early childhood line. Attractive IAS flannel-board stories are available in Spanish/English. The stories are accompanied by the flannelized cutouts. Discussion questions are also included. IAS *Parent Letters* accompanying each of the lessons in the *I Am Special* program are now available in both English and Spanish. Write: Our Sunday Visitor, 200 Noll Plaza, Huntington, IN 46750. Toll-free number: 1-800-348-2440.

PROGRAMS

Children of Divorce: A Resource

If you are looking for a program that helps your students deal with divorce, check out *Living with Divorce*, by Elizabeth Garigan and Michael Urbanski. There are two workbooks in this program, one for children four to ten years old and one for children eleven to eighteen years old. It is designed to help you talk with children and young people and help them work through their feelings of anger, guilt, and pain. Very practical. It is published by Sheed and Ward. Workbooks cost $6.95 each.

Sexuality Education Resource for Parents

The Family Enrichment Bureau has produced a new sexuality education program entitled *Understanding Our Sexuality*. It consists of three audiotapes and a guidebook for parents and/or educators for use in providing sexuality education for children from fifth through eighth grade. It is designed to be used by parents in the home or with small groups of youth. Check it out. It is a good program to promote if parents are looking for help in this area. If you have a home-school organization, you may ask them to investigate it. Cost is $30 for one set, with discounts for multiple orders. Write: Family Enrichment Bureau, 1615 Ludington Street, Escanaba, MI 49829-2894. Phone: (906) 786-7002.

Infancy Narratives

The popular Scripture scholar Father Eugene La Verdiere has a series of five tapes on the infancy narratives available through Credence Cassettes, P.O. Box 281, Kansas City, MO 64141. You don't have to be a Scripture scholar yourself to understand and appreciate Father La Verdiere's excellent and easy-to-follow exegesis.

* * *

The National Catholic Education Association has recently published the fruit of its extensive research into parish religious education entitled *Toward Effective Parish Religious Education for Children and Young People: A National Study* ($10.50 for members, $14.50 for nonmembers). Its findings in some instances verify long-held but unsubstantiated beliefs, such as the positive impact the presence of a professional DRE has on a program, the importance of parental involvement, etc. There are also some valuable surprises that are uncovered. But find out for yourself. It is "must reading" for anyone responsible for planning and/or administering parish religious education programs. Order from NCEA Publications, Suite 100, 1077-30th Street, N.W., Washington, DC 20007-9964.

* * *

At this writing the United States Catholic Conference's Commission on Marriage and Family is presently circulating a draft of a study entitled *A Family Perspective in Church and Society*. When the final draft is published, it should become an important resource to anyone responsible for or interested in ministering to the family. Catholic educators will find it especially helpful in coming to better understand and relate to the families of the children they are teaching — and in understanding the children themselves.

MISCELLANEOUS

One of the finest sources for background material for finding out what is available in terms of teaching aids and programs is the United States Catholic Conference, 1312 Massachusetts Avenue, N.W., Washington, DC 20005-4105. A significant number of excellent materials has been developed for both adults and children, including videocassettes, films, and inexpensive printed materials.

* * *

If you are interested in finding out more about the RCIA (Rite of Christian Initiation of Adults) and how it is being implemented in the United States, write to the North American Forum on the Catechumenate, 3017 4th Street, N.E., Washington, DC 20017. The Forum also distributes a wide variety of books and other resources related to the RCIA and publishes a quarterly newsletter. Ask for a list of their materials and prices.

* * *

The Institute for Justice and Peace is an excellent source for teaching materials, background information, and all related resources dealing with peace and justice. For their catalog or for information, write the Institute at 4144 Lindell, No. 400, St. Louis, MO 63108.

* * *

Christian Film and Video is a new bimonthly review and resource guide for video and film materials suitable for religious education. It is published by Curtis Mark Communications, 501 E. Seminary, Wheaton, IL 60187. With the growing availability of video materials, this can be a real aid in alerting you to what is worth pursuing. Suggest that your librarian or DRE subscribe. Cost: $8.00 per year.

Teacher Notes